THE
GOLDEN WILLOW

THE
GOLDEN
WILLOW

The Story of a Lifetime of Love

HARRY BERNSTEIN

BALLANTINE BOOKS / NEW YORK

Copyright © 2009 by Harry Bernstein

Published in the United States by Ballantine Books,
an imprint of The Random House Publishing Group,
a division of Random House, Inc., New York.

BALLANTINE and colophon are registered trademarks
of Random House, Inc.

Library of Congress Cataloging-in-Publication Data
Bernstein, Harry.
The golden willow : the story of a lifetime of love / Harry Bernstein.
p. cm.
ISBN 978-0-345-51102-7 (alk. paper)
1. Bernstein, Harry, 1910–   2. Bernstein, Harry, 1910—Marriage.
3. Authors, American—20th century—Biography.   4. Jews—United
States—Biography.   I. Title.
PS3552.E7345Z46 2009
818'.54—dc22
[B]   2009002146

Printed in the United States of America on acid-free paper

www.ballantinebooks.com

2 4 6 8 9 7 5 3 1

First Edition

Book design by Susan Turner

To Ruby and Charles and Adraenne

THE
GOLDEN WILLOW

Chapter One

2000

On the morning of my ninetieth birthday I awoke very early and to a rather strange experience. The moment I opened my eyes I was blinded by a curtain of dancing, dazzling spots of light of different colors and shapes. They sometimes merged into one another, forming new shapes and sizes and colors, and never remained still. It was like looking through a kaleidoscope, and not at all unpleasant, and so I remained still for a while, looking into this magic, surrounded by a deep silence that was broken only by the sound of birds singing outside in the garden.

And as I did so, a curious thought ran through my head: that this was how the world was at the very beginning, before people came, just these colors and this deep silence, and nothing else.

Then I shifted my head slightly on the pillow, and the phenomenon vanished instantly. It was, after all, only the sun bursting through the window and stabbing right into my eyes. I could now lie with everything quite normal, and I was careful not to shift about too much lest I disturb my wife, who was sleeping quietly at my side, her still-dark hair tumbled about her head on the pillow, her breathing light and barely audible.

I lay there listening to the sound of the birds singing outside, one bird seeming to dominate all the others with its sweet, trilling notes—a mockingbird, I have no doubt. It was altogether a pleasant spring day, and I could not have wanted anything better for my birthday. Yet as my thoughts came awake, I was conscious of a certain heaviness growing inside me.

I was suddenly becoming aware of the fact that I was ninety years old that day, and that in turn gave my mind a morbid twist, for ninety was old, it was very old. At one time I would have considered anyone of that age as good as dead. Certainly it was the end of things. And what had I done in all those years to justify my existence? I had wanted to be a writer. But the best I had done so far were some short stories published in little magazines that few people read, some freelance writing for newspaper Sunday supplement magazines, and a short novel published by a small press that nobody had read except myself and the publisher, who went bankrupt right after he published my book. True, I had written dozens of other novels, but none of them had ever been published.

I thought of all that as I lay there that morning, and gloom swept over me. It was too late now. I could never be the writer I had wanted to be. There was nothing really to celebrate about this birthday.

Then I heard a faint stirring at my side. I turned my head a little. It was my wife. She was still sleeping, but was evidently in the process of beginning to awaken. As I looked at her and listened to her quiet breathing, I thought, *Well, here's some compensation for all the things I haven't done.* I had married her in 1935, during the Depression, and I'd had a wonderful life with her.

I remembered something of those early days, and a smile came to my face. Our first home was a furnished room in a brownstone on West 68th Street, and it was there one day, while we were still in the passionate throes of our honeymoon, that I led Ruby to the mirror that hung over the dresser.

I told her to look into it, and I stepped behind her, took both her cheeks between my fingers, and pulled, distorting the lovely features.

"When you are older, maybe sixty or seventy"—who could get older than that?—"you may look like this," I said, "but I'll love you as much then as I do now."

Well, I had kept my promise: I did love her as much now as I had then. But she never looked the way I had predicted. In my eyes, she was as beautiful now as the day I had met her, at a dance in Webster Hall in New York. She was only a year younger than I, and yet her features showed only the slightest wrinkling, and her hair was still mostly dark, with only a few touches of gray here and there.

Then I realized that she was awake and was looking up at me with her large, dark eyes, and she was smiling.

"Happy birthday, darling," she whispered, and I bent and kissed her.

Yes, I had a lot to be thankful for, and it took some of the gloom away. Besides, it was truly a lovely day, just perfect for a celebration, bright and sunny and gently warm. And at this time of the year the retirement community in New Jersey in which we lived was at its best, the streets decorated with rows of ornamental trees in full bloom, row after row of dazzling white blossoms. The flowers were out everywhere, the tulips, the daffodils, the irises, and wherever you went, you caught the rich fragrance of lilacs.

Our garden was at its best too, with our cherry tree a mass of pink, the dogwood delicately white, and the mock orange pure white also and giving off its orange-like fragrance so deep and rich it made you hold your breath. But it was our golden willow that held your attention, giant in the center of the garden with its long, thin branches billowing out into the shape of an old-fashioned ball gown, with some of the branches trailing along the ground gracefully.

The golden willow was the first tree we had planted when we came here to live, and Ruby and I had good reason for doing that, only it was a secret that we kept to ourselves. A mere thin sapling when we put it in the ground, it had grown to a tremendous size, outstripping all the other trees in the garden, standing big and beautiful in the center of them all, a shining gold centerpiece. It attracted immediate attention as we led our guests out onto the lawn that day to loll in the sun on the lawn chairs we'd set out and to sip drinks before dinner.

When our grandchildren were younger, they used to play hide-and-seek in the willow tree, and Ruby and I, watching them, would cast amused glances at each other, knowing well the hiding places in that tree. It was part of our secret. But the grandchildren were older now, too old to play, old enough to be able to join us for drinks.

Well, everybody was older that day, and there were fewer guests than there had been at previous birthdays. They had been dwindling for several years now, our relatives and friends dropping off one by one. Our son, Charles, and his wife were there with their adult children, as were our daughter, Adraenne, and her husband, and two or three still surviving friends, a relatively small number compared to what there used to be at previous gatherings.

Dinner was held as usual at the Harvest, a favorite restaurant of ours, and the Polish proprietress, a tall, thin, bony woman with a pronounced accent, whom we knew well from years of dining there, had insisted on making it a special early Thanksgiving dinner, complete with turkey and all the trimmings.

"For you," she had said to me when we were ordering the dinner, "it must be a Thanksgiving party. You are ninety. Not many people come to be ninety. So we give thanks to God."

It was an extraordinarily good dinner, a regular feast, and jolly enough, but not as jolly as previous birthday parties, and I missed two of our good friends who had died the past year, Ann and Pete Warth, with whom we had gone to Europe once, and whom we'd seen almost every day—both of them in that same year gone. And another was my younger brother, Sidney. All my other brothers and sisters had died in the past few years, and I had fully expected that Sidney, who was ten years younger than I, would outlive me. But no, he too had gone, and I was the only one left in my family.

I thought of that in the midst of all the jollity at the dinner table, and I felt a heaviness inside me, but was careful not to show it to Ruby or any of our guests.

The highlight of the party came with their serving of the birthday cake. The proprietress herself carried the cake in, leading a procession of waiters all singing "Happy Birthday." She placed it in front of me, while those at our table and the other tables around us all cheered. There were nine tall candles burning in the top of the mountainous multilayered cake, each one representing a decade, and I was to blow them out—if possible, in one breath. That was my intention, and it would show them that I still had strength enough to do the job. I bent down over the cake and blew as hard as I could, but all that happened was that the flames on the candles flickered to one side but remained lit. I blew again, and the same thing happened. There were encouraging shouts, and I tried but failed once more. Amidst all the shouting and laughter, one of my younger grandchildren, Pete, slipped over to my side, saying, "Let me help you, Grandpa."

He bent down beside me, pursed his lips, and blew, and all the candles went out. Cheers went up, and more laughter, and I had to laugh with them. I thanked Pete, hiding the mortification I felt, and cut the first slice of cake. I tried to forget what had happened. But it was the first time in all my birthdays that I had failed to blow out the candles on a birthday cake, and it hurt.

WE SAW OUR GUESTS off that evening. It had grown dark by then, but it was still early. We stood outside and waved to them as they drove off in their cars. Then we started to turn to go back into the house, but stopped. It was a lovely evening and there was a full moon out, big and bright in a sky filled with stars. I think it reminded us of something, another evening like that. But neither of us said anything about that.

"Would you like to go for a walk?" I asked.

"Yes." Ruby spoke instantly. She loved walking, as I did, especially on evenings like this when it was just too pleasant to be indoors. The weather, in fact, seemed to have grown warmer, and it was almost a summery warmth, so there'd be no need for me to go in and get her a wrap of some sort against any evening coolness.

Ordinarily, a walk would have meant going around the lake, which was at the foot of our street and had a path that was a little more than a mile in circumference, just long enough for an evening stroll. But instead of turning to the right toward the lake

I turned in the opposite direction and led her with me. She was puzzled.

"Where are we going?" she said.

"You'll see," I said.

It wasn't far. I led her to our garden at the back of the house, and there was the golden willow I had brought her to see, shining and more beautiful than ever in the moonlight, as I had expected it would be. And more than that: It was a duplicate of the one we had seen in Central Park so many years ago, which had inspired us to plant this one.

The feeling for that night was strong in me. It had been a long time ago, before Ruby and I were married. It was the summer we had met one hot night at a dance. I had no job then, and no money, so I couldn't take her to theaters or places where it cost money, and Central Park was free. Ruby didn't care so long as we were together, and she went with me gladly to the park almost every night. There were band concerts on some days, and outdoor dancing on others, and there was always the zoo, and perhaps best of all, the benches hidden in the shadow of trees.

That night we had gone to the band concert, and we sat listening for a while, then became restless. It was a night like tonight, a full moon in the sky, stars everywhere, and we slipped away and began strolling hand in hand along the path that borders the lake there, pausing now and then to kiss. Suddenly, we saw it from a distance, towering over all the other trees, its golden leaves shining in the moonlight. We had never seen one before, and its beauty took our breath away. We went up to it and stood looking at it closely for a while, then I parted some of the branches and we stepped inside. It was like entering some holy place. It made me think of a cathedral, with its high ceiling formed around the thick trunk. Ruby and I stood looking at each other in the dark, and then I put my arms around her and drew her to me, and then we were lying on a bed of soft, rotted branches that had formed around the base of the tree over the years, and we could hear the band playing in the distance, and it was there we had our first lovemaking.

Well, it all came back to me as I stood looking at our willow bathed in the moonlight in our garden, and I suddenly found myself parting the branches of the tree with one hand while holding Ruby's hand with the other.

"What are we doing?" Ruby whispered, looking around, fearful that some of our neighbors might be watching.

I didn't answer. I knew what I was doing. I tried to lead her in. "Come on," I whispered back.

"Are you crazy?" she said.

"No, I'm not," I said. "Please come in with me."

"Do you realize," she said, "you're ninety years old?"

"Yes. That's why I want to go in."

She came with me into the tree. Perhaps I had been thinking also of trying and failing to blow out those candles on the birthday cake. Perhaps some of the sting had remained. But I think it was more than that. It was the moonlight too, and the recollection of that night in Central Park. Our bed was as soft as the one there. Many years of rotted branches and leaves had accumulated, and the loamy smell was strong in our nostrils. We slept afterward, close together, our arms wrapped around each other.

Chapter Two

A LOW GROWL OF THUNDER AND A FLASH OF LIGHTNING WOKE US UP. We scrambled quickly to our feet, ducked out of the tree, and ran for the house, reaching it just in time as the first drops of rain began to fall.

We were laughing and happy at our escape because the storm came in full force soon after we had entered, with crashes of thunder and violent streaks of lightning. We wasted no time getting into bed. It was a good chorus for sleep and I think we rather enjoyed it, lying there once again close together listening to the thunder and seeing the lightning zigzag across the sky through the window. Then after one bolt of lightning there was a sudden crash of something heavy falling.

"What's that?" Ruby whispered.

"I don't know," I whispered back.

I was not inclined to go and look, and we both gave up worrying and were soon asleep.

It was quiet and sunny when we woke up the next morning. It was a day similar to the one I had awakened to twenty-four hours earlier, the morning of my ninetieth birthday. I was ninety and a day, I reflected, yawning. But the storm was over, and I wondered how much damage it had done.

Ruby was the first out of bed. I was still lying there when I heard her cry out, "Oh, my God."

"What's the matter?" I shot up in bed.

"Come take a look!"

She was standing looking through the window, horror on her face. I quickly joined her at the window, and I gave a cry myself. Our beautiful golden willow was lying stretched out full length on the ground in a mass of golden leaves and branches, its roots torn out of the earth and protruding upward with lumps of dark earth clinging to them. It lay there like a fallen giant killed in battle.

That tree had meant so much to both of us, and I could see that Ruby was in tears. I put my arm around her and tried to comfort her. "You'll get over it," I said. "After all, it's only a tree."

But as far as she was concerned, it could have been a person. "There'll never be another one like that tree," she said. "Can we plant another one?"

I laughed. "Ruby, darling," I said, "I could no more replace a tree as beautiful as that one as I could you."

"I love your compliment," she said, in a muffled voice and holding a tissue to her eyes, "but are you sure we couldn't plant another?"

"I'm quite sure," I said. "You know how long it took for us to get that one to grow. I've almost forgotten. About thirty years? Maybe forty? But don't worry," I hastened to add, "we've got lots of time left for both of us."

"Have we?" she said, but she spoke absently, as if her mind had struck something else.

"Yes," I said confidently, "lots of it, lots and lots."

It seemed that way for two more years, with Ruby's anemia that had recently begun, apparently under control, enabling her to continue teaching her yoga class every Wednesday morning at the clubhouse, looking as lithe, slender, and shapely as ever in her leotard, even though she had joined me as a nonagenarian. The two of us enjoyed life together, even making two more trips to Mexico, which had been our winter home for years.

She was ninety-one and I was ninety-two when we decided to celebrate our sixty-seventh wedding anniversary. Our children, Charlie and Adraenne, got together and arranged it for us at their expense, an anniversary gift that couldn't have been better for us: a two-night stay at the Plaza Hotel in New York, close to Central Park, where we had spent our honeymoon, and near where we had lived for the first few months of our marriage; orchestra seats for *La Bohème*, our favorite opera, at the Met; and a string quartet concert at Carnegie Hall. What more could we have wanted?

We drove to the Plaza in our car for the two nights of luxury and found ourselves immediately in a world we'd never known before: a uniformed concierge to greet us, a bellboy to take our keys and park the car, another bellboy to take our bags, a thickly carpeted lobby to cross on our way to the desk to register, then an elevator up to our room, and what a room! It was large and handsomely furnished, and yes, it overlooked the park, a perfect view that drew our attention immediately. But not as much as the canopied bed. This fairly made us gasp. We had seen canopied beds before only in movies. Our kids had thought of everything.

The next two days went by too fast for us. We could easily have overcome our awe and adjusted very nicely to life at the Plaza: people waiting on us hand and foot; sumptuous meals in a restaurant where two or three waiters, including a wine steward with a large key dangling around his neck, hovered over us; a stroll in the park, a wonderful opera at night, and a string quartet the following night— all of this we could easily have embraced for the rest of our lives.

But before it was over we gave ourselves another treat. We would go back to West 68th Street and see the old brownstone where we had lived for several months after we were married. It would make a perfect ending to our anniversary celebration.

Fortunately, the weather had been good to us during these two days, warm and sunny, as pleasant as we could have wanted it. It was like that when we set out on the pilgrimage to our former home. Years ago it would have taken us just a few minutes to walk from 59th Street to 68th, and it would have been nothing at all. But these were different, older years, and we went slowly, and soon had to rest on one of the benches that lined Central Park West. We had already discovered in our strolls through the park that we were no longer able to walk at a brisk pace and had to have frequent rests, so this came as no surprise to us, and we were grateful for the benches that were so plentiful.

But at last, perspiring a good deal from the sun that was less pleasant than when we had started out, we passed the big white stone building of the Ethical Culture Society, where we had spent many Sunday mornings listening to Algernon Black preach and lecture, and came to 68th Street.

We smiled at each other as we turned into it. The street was much the same as it had been sixty-seven years ago, with the two rows of brownstones all exactly alike facing each other across the street, their high stoops slanting down uniformly to the sidewalk. Nothing seemed to have changed, and we were glad of that. When you go back into the past you want everything to be the same. Nostalgia came over us as we walked slowly up the block, looking this way and that for familiar things: the flower boxes that some of the houses used to display at windowsills, the dentist's sign in the dusty window at number 42. Well, there had been changes. The flower boxes were gone, and so were the For Rent signs that used to appear in so many of the windows, and there was no more dentist sign nor he himself, an elderly, frowsy man who'd seemed to spend more of his time puttering around the place fixing his decaying property than he did at dentistry. We'd rarely seen patients going into his place, and the sign in the window had been curled and yellowed with age, like the dentist himself.

We came to our house finally, close to the end of the block, near Columbus Avenue, and our hearts beat a little faster as we saw it, still standing there, the same house we had come to that spring day carrying our two suitcases that contained all the belongings we had in the world. Two young people, very much excited with our new life, very much in love. As we mounted the steps I imagined I saw our landlady looking at us through the window of the ground-floor apartment where she lived with her daughter. Her name was Mrs. Janeski, but we had already dubbed her Madame Janeski because of the haughty, aristocratic manner she affected when we came to rent the room, informing us that she took in only the "best" kind of people. Her sharp scrutiny had indicated that she was not at all sure about us yet.

But Ruby and I were thinking of something else as we stood there looking at the house. It was Ruby who spoke first.

"I wonder if the plumber ever came," she said.

"I wonder," I said, and we both laughed.

I had been thinking of exactly the same thing, and this wasn't surprising. It had been on our minds often during the time we had stayed at Madame Janeski's place, the only fly in the ointment. It was a lovely room as furnished rooms went in those days. It was just perfect for us, but it lacked one thing—a shower. There was a bathtub, a quite nice one, but that one all-important attachment, the shower, was missing, and it was essential to both of us.

Madame Janeski had seemed shocked when we brought it up to her, as if she had not known until then that there was no shower in the bathroom. She would attend to it right away, she said. She would call her plumber and have him come and install one.

The plumber had not come, and Madame Janeski had a ready excuse: his daughter had suffered an accident, and he'd had to rush to the hospital where she'd been taken. But he would come next week. And the next week, when the plumber still failed to arrive, it was because he had fallen down the church steps and fractured a leg. Her excuses were endless, and we finally realized that if the plumber really existed, the reasons for his failure to show up were the products of her imaginative mind.

All of that came back to us as we stood there in front of our former home, and we were laughing over it when the front door opened and a short, rather stocky man wearing blue jeans and a checkered flannel shirt came out. He had been watching us through the window, the same one through which Madame Janeski used to observe us suspiciously as we went in and out, and he was curious.

"Is there anything I can do for you?" he asked courteously.

Ruby and I looked at each other. The same thing was on our minds. We would have liked to go in and see our old room. I explained to him why we were here, to pay a sentimental visit to the first place in which we had lived together, and that it was our sixty-seventh wedding anniversary. He was understanding and quite pleasant about it. He was the new owner of the house, a fairly recent purchase. He was also, despite the jeans and flannel shirt, a professor of economics at New York University, and it would be no trouble at all to show us the room.

"Although," he explained, "we don't call it a furnished room anymore. It's a studio apartment."

We smiled and thought it probably rented for ten times or more what we'd paid for it. Fortunately for us, the person who had the studio apartment was away for the weekend. We followed the man into the house, and everything was familiar to us: the hallway, the little table where the mailman used to leave the mail (with my returned manuscripts among the letters), the carpeted stairs. It was not as spic and span as when Madame Janeski ran the place, however, and the banister did not shine with polishing.

We went up the one flight, and there we were, and the landlord was fumbling in his pocket for the key. He opened the door and stood aside to let us in. We both hesitated. A recollection had come to us of how I had carried Ruby over the threshold, and I think we both wished we could do it again. But it would have been a bit too much in front of this man who was waiting for us to go in, and I doubt if I would have had the strength to pick Ruby up and carry her in.

We entered, and it was an emotional moment for both of us as we stood there looking around at what had once been our first home. It was the same as it had been then, sun-filled, the two windows looking out onto the garden below and the row of backyards with lawn chairs set out for loungers, and clotheslines strung across on which I used to hang out my wash, surreptitiously, keeping watch for observers.

There still was the little alcove with the dressing table that Ruby had treasured so much, a touch of elegance that rarely came with a furnished room. Over the dressing table was the mirror that I'd had Ruby look into while I distorted her features and told her that was how she might look when she got old, but I'd love her as much as I did in our twenties. And there was the bathroom.

We looked at each other. Did we dare?

"May we go into the bathroom?" I asked the landlord.

He nodded, but I think he was startled when both of us went in together. Even the most intimate of couples rarely go into a bathroom together. We did, however, and it was not to use it but to look. We looked, and there was no shower—just one of those portable attachments that you buy in the drugstore.

"The plumber never came," I said.

Ruby started to laugh, but I shushed her, and we went out to face the still-puzzled landlord. I said, "There is no real shower in there still. We never had one."

"Oh, didn't you?" he said. "Well, I just took the place over and I haven't got around to making a few improvements. But I expect a plumber in a week or so to put the shower in."

After thanking him for letting us see our old place, out on the street Ruby and I exploded into laughter so hysterical we had to hold on to each other. People stared at us, thinking probably we were drunk.

Well, that was our sixty-seventh wedding anniversary, a happy one, as happy as every day had been in all those years.

And then, one week after we had returned home, we woke up one morning and found blood on Ruby's pillow.

Chapter Three

1935

AT FIRST, WHEN WE WERE MARRIED, I HAD NO JOB, AND RUBY DID ALL
the supporting, working as a secretary in the office of Brentano's
bookstore on Fifth Avenue. It was 1935, the height of the Great Depression. Luckily, after a few months, I was able to get a job with
MGM reading books and plays submitted for movie consideration,
and it was then we decided we could afford a place where we had
more space and a proper kitchen and bathroom—with the shower
that we did not have in the furnished room on West 68th Street. We
found an apartment on Bleecker Street, on the top floor of an old
tenement house that had just been renovated. Everything was new
and fresh and still smelled of paint, and to us, our apartment was the
height of luxury and represented a step up in the world. The three-
flight climb was nothing to us. We were young and healthy and we
could take the steps two at a time.

The entire place was occupied by writers, artists, musicians, and dancers, and we felt quite at home among them, except that a singer practicing somewhere in the building, a woman who was studying to be an operatic soprano and who made some awful sounds, annoyed us and probably many others in the building. And there was the modern dancer who lived next door to us and liked to move her furniture around late at night. We never found out why she did this, but the walls were thin and the scraping and thumping sounds of sofa and chairs and tables being dragged across the floor from one place to another came through to us clearly and kept us awake.

Yet, for all this, we loved our new home, and our brand-new, shiny solid maple furniture gave us a lot of pleasure. It was my job to polish it once every week to keep it new-looking, and I did this religiously every Saturday morning while Ruby was still at work in Brentano's, Saturday being a workday then. We had bought the furniture with the help of a friend who knew the head salesman in a large furniture store that specialized in solid maple, which was all the rage then among young couples. We had to ask for Henry, and to tell Henry that Yetta had sent us, and Henry in turn saw to it that we got a big discount.

One of the pieces we bought was a large lounge chair. It had soft cushions and maple arms and legs. I had resisted buying it at first because I thought it was unnecessary and too expensive even with Henry's discount. The salesman was a tall, thin fellow with a melancholy look on his face. He never smiled once, and he carried a notebook in one hand and a pencil in the other and jotted down the things as we bought them and made special notes that we assumed were the discounts that he was giving us. When it came to the discussion as to whether we should buy the lounge chair or not, he turned his head aside as if to indicate his neutrality, with the sad look still on it, and I think I heard him give a sigh.

Ruby and I were arguing, though not as couples usually do. I was telling her that I could well do without the chair, though really I wanted it.

And Ruby was saying, "No, you can't. This isn't luxury. It's a necessity. You need it for your reading."

"Why do I need it for reading?" I asked. "Since when do I read with that part of my body?"

"Stop being funny," she said. "It isn't just for when you read. It's for resting too. I'd love to see you sprawled out in that chair."

"I could use the bed for that," I said. "With you on it."

"Don't be so funny," she said. "We'll buy the chair."

We did, and I did a lot of sprawling out on it. And I loved Ruby more than ever for thinking of it, the way she often did for me in so many other ways.

We were a happy couple. We had a good social life in the Village, though it was often halted by my reading. I did all my work at home, and this sometimes prevented us from having people in for an evening or going to their places. Ruby never minded. She read a great deal herself, except that they were books of her choice, and many an evening passed quietly with both of us immersed in our books.

Still, we managed to visit others, and there were always the soirees at James Deutsch's place on Waverly, the German fellow whom I threatened to kill once when he tried to kiss Ruby at our first gathering there. He had since apologized and become a great friend of ours, and he still was comptroller of a department store by day and a bohemian playwright at night, and held lively soirees—as he preferred to call the gatherings—at night in what he also liked to call his studio, and which could be reached by climbing an iron spiral stairway for three floors. There he drank much Scotch and smoked many cigarettes, and sometimes played Beethoven loudly on his record player and conducted the music at the same time, surrounded by his admirers, who were mostly young females who sat on the floor, watching worshipfully. He wore a beret and an artist's smock then.

There were others we mixed with in the Village. Adolf was a true artist, and a rather good one, I thought. He was perpetually gloomy and could sit for an entire evening with his head cast down, in his hand a glass of wine that he never drank. Perhaps the gloomy state came from his wife, Lucia, a pretty woman with a light complexion that contrasted sharply with Adolf's dark one. Her manner and speech were always theatrical and accompanied by gestures of the hands, and she was forever belittling her husband in front of people with frequent suggestions that he was sexually impotent. Adolf never said a word, just sat there with his head bent and the glass of wine in his hand.

Lucia frequently gave out invitations to people for dinner, or some other occasion at her house, but few people accepted, and those who did almost never found her home when they arrived. Ruby and I knew nothing about that when we were invited to breakfast. We went and they were home, all right, but fast asleep in their bed, and when we had knocked several times Adolf came to the door in his pajamas and sleepily suggested we come back in an hour or so. We never did.

And there were the Grossmans, Ben and Germaine. Ben was a lawyer by day and a playwright at night, and having heard that I was a reader for a moving-picture company, he promptly had Germaine invite us to dinner. Ben was doing well as a lawyer, and they lived in one of the more modern apartment buildings on Greenwich Avenue. It had an elevator that took us up to their apartment on the fifth floor, and Ruby and I were impressed. We had visions of a good, hearty meal, and I was just in the mood for it, and perhaps a couple of drinks to go with it. I'd had a rough day with a mystery novel. I hated mystery novels, and this one deserved my disdain because it was long and complex with numerous red herrings and lots of tiresome repetitions of "Where were you the night of . . . ?"

The warm welcome we got as we entered the apartment and the succulent smell of roast beef emanating from the kitchen were promising. Ben shook my hand several times and told me how glad he was to see me, and we sat down in an expensively furnished living room, but no drinks were served.

"I've got a surprise for you," Ben said. "Excuse me for a moment."

He disappeared briefly and returned holding something in his hand. It was a thick manuscript bound in a purple cover.

"I gave up writing plays and am trying my hand at novels," he said. "I just finished this one. It's a mystery novel, and I thought before we sit down to dinner you might want to glance over it and give me your opinion, and maybe if you think it's any good you'd like to offer it for me to the movie company you're with."

He plopped it down on my lap, grinning affably. I felt its thickness in my hands, and for quite some time I did not say anything. Ruby was sitting beside me, and out of the corner of my eye I could see her expression, which was probably much like my own—a mixture of many things, but mostly disgust.

After a few moments had passed, I said, "I'd like to ask you one question."

"Yes?" He spoke eagerly, thinking I was interested already and wanted to know more about his transition from playwriting to novel writing, or something else connected with the manuscript.

I said, "Could you tell me where the nearest hamburger place is to here?"

A puzzled look now came on his face. "Hamburger!" he said. "What do you want that for?"

"Because that's where Ruby and I are going to have our dinner."

I handed the manuscript back to him. Then I took Ruby's hand and we left.

I HAVE BEEN ASKED many times by reporters during interviews about the marriage that Ruby and I had. Somehow the idea of a flawless marriage that lasted so many years arouses curiosity in a good many people, if not skepticism.

One reporter asked bluntly, "Are you sure there were no bumps in that wonderful marriage of yours?"

I had to say we disagreed at times; what two human beings wouldn't? But it was never anything serious. We had so many things in common—books, music, art, almost everything—and Ruby always maintained an even disposition, a sweetness that never changed, and a smile that was always there. How can one quarrel with a person like that?

Yet there was one time when there was a bump, and a rather serious one. It was about having children. I don't know how the topic came about, but it did, and we discovered that we were at odds on the matter. Ruby wanted to have children; I didn't. I'd been brought up in a family of six children where there was constant wrangling and strife. Even at night in bed there was no rest from it. Three of us were crowded into one bed, and I slept at the feet of my two older brothers. We fought for space, and I got kicked many times. No, I'd had enough of children and wanted none of my own.

With Ruby, it was equally understandable. She had been brought up in a family where there were just two children, and Ruby's younger brother was slightly mentally disabled and was no companion for her. Nor was there a father—he'd died before the two children really knew him. Often, she told me, she envied those of her friends who had large families, and she certainly wanted children of her own—someday.

Yes, someday. It was early in our marriage when that came up, and we were able to push the subject aside without making the bump a serious one. In the meantime, we were enjoying our life in the Village with lots of friends and lots of places to go—the Civic Repertory Theater on Fourteenth Street to watch Eva Le Gallienne in Chekhov's *The Seagull,* Tolstoy's *The Living Corpse,* or any one of dozens of other plays that only this wonderful theater group could put on. For an admission charge of twenty-five cents you could sit in the gallery.

Then sometimes I would go down to Gray's drugstore in Times Square and get on line in their basement to buy discount tickets for some Broadway show. And we'd walk to the theater from the Village, and walk back again, and once, I remember, I chose to halt our walk and pull Ruby close to me and kiss her, and a passing car filled with young fellows slowed down and a head popped through the window and a voice yelled out, "Why don't you marry the girl?"

Our four years in the Village went swiftly and happily, and there was never any more talk of children. The summers were a bit difficult for me. Our apartment on the top floor became an oven, with the sun beating down on the roof directly above us. I still read manuscripts for the movies, though I'd changed from MGM to Twentieth Century Fox, and I sweated over the books and things I had to read. When it came to typing out the synopsis that was required, my fingers were so moist from sweat that they slipped on the keys. I worked stripped to the waist, like a stoker in a furnace room, the sweat pouring over my body. I would keep a basin of cold water nearby, and every so often I would dip a cloth into it and run water over my head and face and chest.

One hot afternoon, as I sat at my desk struggling to finish typing a synopsis of the book I had just read, I heard footsteps coming up the stairs. The door was wide open to let in what little air there was, and the sound came to me clearly. I halted my work, thinking it was one of our neighbors on the floor, perhaps the modern dancer come to move some furniture around and bother me still more. But it wasn't a neighbor. It was Ruby.

I gaped at her at first as she came through the door. Then I noticed that her face was pale, and she didn't look well. Nor had she ever come home from the office this early. I jumped to my feet at once and led her to a chair, and she sank onto it gratefully.

"Aren't you feeling well?" I asked anxiously.

"Not terribly well," she said. "They let me go home early at the office." And then she added—with complete irrelevance, I thought—"Darling, do you remember that joke James told us last Saturday night?"

"Joke?" I said, more puzzled than ever.

"Yes, the one about the unmarried girl who told her mother she wasn't feeling well and said, 'Don't worry, Mother. I'm only a little bit pregnant'?"

I gave a short laugh. "Yes, I remember it. So what?"

"Well," Ruby went on, "that's the way it is with me."

It took me a half second to catch on, and for another brief moment there was shock. But that only lasted another second, and then I was on my knees in front of her. It was a surprising reaction on my part. We'd quarreled over this once. I was dead set against having children. I hated families. I'd been miserable in one for a good part of my life. It had been a family of bickering and poverty and no father to speak of, and I had made it clear to Ruby that I would never have a family of my own.

But in this moment all that had vanished, and I was on my knees in front of her and holding her hands and telling her how wonderful it was.

She was not sure about me, though. She looked at me anxiously and said, "Are you sure you don't mind?"

"No, of course not," I said. "This is great, really great. I do mean it."

I did, without any doubt. And there was something else that had happened once to contradict my feelings about families. It was when I was ten years old. Until then I had been the youngest, the baby in the family. Then I woke up one morning to hear a baby crying in the next room, where my parents slept. My two brothers, who shared the bed with me, woke up too, and they laughed when I asked where the baby had come from.

"He doesn't know anything yet," Saul had sneered.

"He'll find out one day," Joe had added.

Of course I hadn't known. I hadn't noticed my mother getting larger and larger, as they had, knowing what it meant. I went into her bedroom later that day and saw her lying there with the baby at her side, and she motioned to me and said, "Come and see your little brother."

When I looked at the little wrinkled face wrapped in blankets beside her, I'd felt an overwhelming happiness that blotted out all the poisonous feelings I might have had toward this new addition to the family. And it was that same kind of happiness that rose in me to greet the news Ruby brought me that day.

Chapter Four

IT WAS NOTHING TO WORRY ABOUT, THE DOCTOR ASSURED US, JUST A common nosebleed, but our daughter, Adraenne, was not satisfied. She was a nurse practitioner and knowledgeable about medicine, and she knew who were the best doctors. She chose one in New York and made an appointment for Ruby.

It turned out Ruby was suffering from anemia, but one that could be controlled with a weekly injection of a medication called Procrit.

Since Adraenne was unable to make the trip to New Jersey from Brooklyn, where she lived, to give Ruby the weekly injection, we turned to our next-door neighbor for help. Blake had been a medic in the army before he retired, and was well trained in giving injections. He was only too glad to oblige, and every Sunday morning he would be at our door, often bringing a cake that his wife, Hildegarde, had baked for us, or perhaps a pot of her delightful chicken soup. Those Sunday mornings became a social event, with sometimes Hildegarde accompanying her husband.

Eventually, I learned to give the injections myself, and they seemed to be working. Blood tests showed that the hemoglobin count was rising, and bit by bit it reached a normal level. The danger had passed. The anemia was not developing into the unmentionable leukemia, as in many cases it did. We were all happy, Ruby especially.

"Now," she said to me when the normal level was reached, "you can take me to the prom."

The Senior Prom was a new innovation in town. All seniors had been invited. It was to be held at the newly opened Cultural Arts Center. High school students were to be the hosts and hostesses. A dinner would be served. There would be a live band for dancing. It had been prominently advertised in the local paper, and Ruby had wanted to go, but I had held back. It seemed just a bit too silly to try to recover the high school days, and I wasn't keen on dancing, especially now that I was in my nineties, as was Ruby also.

"Can't we go somewhere else?" I asked Ruby. "How about a play or a good movie?"

"No, I want to go to the prom," she said.

So we went, putting on our best clothes. Ties and jackets required, the invitation had said, and I knew I was going to be uncomfortable wearing a tie and jacket, something I hadn't done in a long time. I must say, though, that Ruby looked beautiful in a blue sleeveless gown that she'd bought specially for the occasion, and no one would have guessed that she was ninety.

It was a long time since we had gone dancing. Perhaps that was true of a great many of the others who came. By the time we arrived, the parking lot was packed and I had to cruise around quite a bit before I could find a vacant parking spot to squeeze into. Two young girls dressed in fancy party gowns greeted us at the door with smiles, and one of them escorted us inside.

It was already crowded and noisy inside, with people seated at large round tables. Our hostess had trouble finding places for us, but she did at last at a table where three other couples were seated. We introduced ourselves, and there were handshakes and curious looks at us.

All of them, it seemed to me, were on the youngish side compared to us. They were sizing us up, probably trying to figure out our age. It wasn't long before one of the women asked us, "If you don't mind telling me, how old are you two?"

When I told them that I was ninety-one and Ruby ninety, there were astonished looks on their faces and cries of "Oh, I don't believe it."

I smiled, and Ruby smiled. We were used to this by now. It had happened before when we were among strangers. Sooner or later they would be saying, "God bless you!" and expressing the hope that when they got to that age, God willing, they hoped they would look half as young as we did.

They did say exactly that. And then, in the midst of the dinner that was being served by the student hosts and hostesses, the band struck up a tune. It was one of the old fox trots, and it was a good opportunity to get away from the table. I took Ruby's hand and we both got up. The others remained seated, and I knew it was because they wanted to see how we would dance—or if we could. I could feel their eyes on us as we went onto the dance floor. Ruby noticed it, too. I said to her, "Let's give them a treat and collapse onto the floor. I'm sure they're expecting it."

"We'll do no such thing," she said. "Instead, give me a few extra twirls and show them how good we are."

I tried. I did my best, but after the second dance I had to beg Ruby for a rest. "I'm bushed," I said. "I really can't do another, otherwise those people at the table are going to get what they expect and I'll have to be carried out."

A bit to my surprise, she said, "All right, darling, let's sit down. To tell you the truth, I'm a bit tired myself."

I don't know if she was telling the truth or not, but we went back to the table and got applause from our neighbors there, and words of praise, and a repetition of how they couldn't believe we were that old.

We left shortly afterward. I couldn't handle the dinner, anyway. It was spaghetti and meatballs, and it got all over my blue serge suit. But mostly it was because we were both very tired.

It was the last time Ruby and I danced together.

Chapter Five

1939

KNICKERBOCKER VILLAGE WAS A HUGE COMPLEX OF MULTISTORY brick buildings in lower Manhattan, close to the East River and the Williamsburg Bridge. Our new apartment was on the tenth floor, overlooking a courtyard. It had two bedrooms, and this chiefly was our reason for moving. Now that Ruby was going to have a baby—despite the fact that she was only a little bit pregnant—we realized immediately that our place in the Village was not large enough to accommodate the extra person who was coming. Nor did we think Greenwich Village was an ideal place in which to bring up a child.

And perhaps too, Ruby and I were changing a little and growing more mature in our thinking. We had met a lot of interesting people there, but we felt that a quieter, more conventional environment would be better suited for our growing family. There was another reason. Ruby had changed her job at Brentano's for one with the government at much better pay. She worked now in the Treasury Building in the Wall Street district, and she would be able to walk there in less than half an hour, something she preferred to crowding onto a subway.

In Knickerbocker Village there were elevators to go up and down—no more stair climbing. And there was a separate bedroom, which would be the baby's room, and which we furnished in advance with a crib and dresser. There was a garden below, with benches to sit on, and other young couples like ourselves, some who already had children, others who were expecting them, as we were. There was a friendly, congenial atmosphere that we liked, and no more thumping when the modern dancer began her mysterious furniture moving late at night.

Ruby's pregnancy was scarcely noticeable while she was dressed, people marveling when they learned the month she was in. Then one unseasonably hot night in September, we came home from a movie and had scarcely opened the door of the apartment and entered into the hallway before Ruby gave a cry and I heard a trickling sound. There was water on the floor around her.

"Quick," she said, as I rushed to help her to a chair. "Call the doctor."

I did while she sat on a wet chair. It was a day when doctors answered calls immediately. His voice came at once, and after I'd told him what had happened, he said, "The water bag has burst. Get her to the hospital at once."

I led Ruby outside, and we were lucky: There was an empty elevator waiting. In a few minutes we were down and outside on Monroe Street looking for a cab. Luck again: A cab pulled up, and I bundled Ruby into it. Soon we were at Beth David Hospital, and Ruby was taken from me, and Dr. Hibbard was taking me aside and saying things that weren't exactly comforting. "I have to tell you this," he said. "We're going to try for a normal delivery, but it's possible she might need a cesarean, and in that case, there'll be some risk. So you have to be prepared."

I wanted to stay, but he urged me to go home and wait until I heard from him. I'll never know why he made it sound so dramatic. Cesareans were common enough even in that day, and there were relatively few fatalities. But anyway, it gave me a sleepless night, and I got up once during the night and sat at the window looking out at the few lighted windows still on in the courtyard, imagining all sorts of things. It was the first time in our married life that we had been separated, and perhaps even under more normal circumstances I would have been sleepless without her.

But that night I went through all sorts of misery, with the doctor's warning sounding in my ears, and thoughts of how I could go on living if Ruby died. I would find out someday, and I would not be far wrong in what my apprehensions were that night. But that was not the time for it. Nor, when I think back on it, had there been any reason for that doctor to have put such fear into me.

Early the next morning my phone rang, and Dr. Hibbard's voice came over sounding more cheerful and optimistic. There had been a cesarean, and Ruby had come out of it quite well, and so had the baby, and it was a boy weighing eight pounds. Congratulations!

I rushed to the hospital, and some of my joy vanished when I looked through a glass screen and saw my son for the first time. His face was a mass of red wrinkles and he was crying.

The intern at my side laughed at my expression. "Don't worry," he said. "We all look like that when we're born, but we all change."

He was right, of course, and I was reassured about Ruby. She was smiling when I came in to see her, and lifted up her arms to me,

and for the brief moment in which we were together again we forgot
even the baby. But not for long. The serenity and complete absorp-
tion in each other that had marked our life before this was gone, and
there was another person with whom we shared all this—one who
was demanding, cried a great deal, had to be fed at regular intervals,
and kept us up at night.

There was much to be done in this new life of ours, and we were
fortunate in having Aunt Lily there to break us in on the caring of
our infant. She and her husband, Peo, had come from Chicago to
live permanently in New York, and Aunt Lily had become a fully
qualified infant nurse. She gave us her services for a week as her gift
to us, and as soon as we arrived home from the hospital she donned
her white uniform and took charge. It was through her that we
learned how to hold the baby so that we did not injure him, how to
bathe him and diaper him and do the many other things that were
necessary. But the week afterward we were on our own. Ruby had no
difficulty becoming a mother, and I know she loved every moment
of it. It was then too she began her album that recorded in great de-
tail the baby's growth and development.

I was the photographer. I took the pictures, mostly with a
Brownie box camera, of the baby lying in bed, the baby kicking his
feet, the baby smiling for the first time, the baby grasping a rattle in
his tiny hand. The album is gone now, along with a good many other
things of the past, but I can remember it so clearly with its badly
taken snapshots and the captions under each one written by Ruby in
white lettering: "Charlie laughed for the first time today . . . Charlie
can now sit up . . . Charlie sneezed and I am afraid he might have a
cold—I must take him to see Dr. Walsh . . ."

Dr. Walsh was our pediatrician and had her office in Knickerbocker Village. The white-haired, soft-spoken woman examined her

squalling, squirming patients with minute care, never the slightest bit ruffled by their antics, going over carefully every inch of the little body, and giving her findings and instructions in a lengthy report that covered at least two sheets of paper.

Charlie grew bigger and continued to develop. The intern had been right: The wrinkles disappeared and the face became quite normal. In fact, we thought it was a lovely face. And one day Ruby reported in her album, "Charlie laughed for the first time today."

On that same day the newspaper headlines blazed, "GERMAN PLANES BOMB LONDON."

THE WAR HAD BEEN RAGING in Europe for over a year. Hitler's armies were sweeping over the continent, taking country after country, and now his planes were blitzing London. In the United States there was talk of the war spreading here, and there was controversy over whether we should or should not get into it.

At Knickerbocker Village, though, the talk was mostly about babies. At least that was so among the mothers; the men might have been talking among themselves about the draft and the possibility that they might be called up. But as the mothers wheeled their babies around the lawns or sat on benches, rocking the carriages to get the crying babies to sleep, the danger of losing their men was still distant, and the conversations that took place dealt with sleepless nights, diarrhea, and breast-feeding or bottles. Ruby mixed well with these people, and we were both quite content with our new surroundings and our new first baby.

Ruby got along with everybody, and everybody liked her, and she made a wonderful mother, as she was with everything. She loved the baby. She loved breast-feeding, and she loved every moment she spent with the baby, even getting up at night to change his diaper or to do whatever was necessary to halt his crying.

I think it was a sad day for her when her maternity leave was over and she had to go back to work. Although she never complained or even said a word to me about it, I know it was not easy for her to relinquish the baby's care to the young Czech woman we had hired to take her place during the day. I have thought about that often, and with a touch of guilt that I also felt then, regretting that I did not make enough money to enable her to stay home permanently. I was still a reader and in the low-pay rut, and still writing and hoping that I would get a book published, even though the country was working its way out of the Depression and jobs were available. But what skill did I have? All I knew was how to read and write, and I did not know how to write well enough to make a living out of it.

But I don't remember glooming over it, and both Ruby and I were quite pleased with Stella. I'm sure she was not more than eighteen, but she took care of the baby while Ruby was away, cooked our meals—quite well too—cleaned the house, and did everything else there was to do, all for forty dollars a month, the going rate at that time for a full-time live-in maid.

No, there was nothing to gloom over. In fact, we were happier than ever with our baby. Ruby was one of those rare women who enjoyed both her job and her home. She rushed to get to the office on time, walking the distance with the zest she had for exercise, and she rushed to get back to her home and her baby, and she was always cheerful about everything.

The only thing that troubled us was the soot. It came from all the surrounding factories, and it crept into the house and had to be cleaned off windowsills and furniture every day. Outside it was even worse. When we took Charlie out in the carriage we made sure that we had clean cloths to wipe off the soot that would soon settle on his face.

I recall one time when I took Charlie out in the carriage on a Sunday afternoon to give Ruby a rest and let her sleep longer, and I sat on a bench next to a young couple with two children. I had seen them before this and had noticed then that they generally sat alone and did not get into conversations with other people. As a result, there was no greeting between us. But when I saw black spots settling on the baby's face I began searching in the carriage for the cloth to wipe his face, and there was none. I had forgotten to take it. The woman saw my problem and promptly offered me a tissue, which I took, thanking her. I did not know their names, and later asked someone who had lived in Knickerbocker a long time what their names were.

What he said meant nothing to me then: Ethel and Julius Rosenberg. They would be in headlines later in every newspaper in the country, a couple charged with spying for the Soviet Union, found guilty in a sensational trial, and finally executed.

But it was the soot that finally drove us away from Knickerbocker Village and from the city itself. We wanted fresher, cleaner air, and we would also need still more space for the second child we would have in the future. So after much soul-searching and examination of our finances, and overcoming the fear and responsibility of owning property, we bought a house in the part of Queens called Laurelton. It was a square brick house, very unattractive-looking, the same as all the other houses around it, but it had lots of room, and it proved to be a good home in the years that we would live there.

OUR FIRST NIGHT IN THE HOUSE was disturbed by a loud voice awakening us, a voice that barked, "Mark time, march! Hup, hup. Forward march! Right, left, halt!"

Startled, we got out of bed and looked out of the window. A full moon was out illuminating our backyard and the one next to us, and there we saw a short, stocky man dressed in a World War I uniform, marching up and down with a rifle over one shoulder. It was our next-door neighbor, Mr. Way, first name unknown.

Afterward, we would discover that this same scene would be repeated by the same individual on every moonlit night, and from other neighbors we would learn that this had been going on ever since they all moved into the development a few years ago. No one ever spoke to him, even though he was more normal during the day. But he was always too busy to talk. His backyard was a jungle of tall weeds, and he worked among them on his hands and knees, pulling some of the weeds up and transplanting them in different places.

At one time his wife and son had lived with him, and during that time there had been the noise of constant fighting, shouting, and screams; several times the police had to be called, and Mr. Way had been taken away. Eventually he returned, and soon the same thing would be repeated. But finally the wife and son left, and there was peace at night save on the moonlit nights when he began his military drills in the backyard.

So this was the one big drawback to the brick bungalow we had bought. Certainly, however, we could not have complained about other neighbors, who became good friends of ours in the years that followed. Nor could we have found any fault with the scenic view from our front windows. Right across the street from us was a small vegetable farm that gave us an immense amount of pleasure.

At one time, not too many years before we came there, the entire area had been farming country. Then the developers came along and bought them up one after another. The land was cheap and houses were in demand, and developers lost no time putting up their rows of look-alike brick houses. But the farm across the street remained because its owner, a tall, stooped, taciturn man, was a stubborn Dutchman by the name of Schmidt, who refused to give up what had been in his family for two or three generations. He rarely talked to any of us and I don't think he cared much for our presence, but we certainly liked his, and from our front windows or from the steps of our house we would watch him plowing the land in the early spring. He still used a horse to pull the plow, and when our children were young they delighted in watching him steer the tired old nag from furrow to furrow.

Then came the pleasure of seeing the thin green shoots come up out of the earth in their straight rows. He had modernized enough to have a sprinkler system put in, so showers of water waved back and forth over the rows of growing vegetables. It was a never-ending feast for the eyes. It made us think that we were out in the country. And soon it was harvest time, and the same groups of foreign women appeared on the scene every year, wearing colored bandanas around their foreheads and dressed in colorful native costumes. They would kneel in the rows and pull out the vegetables, jabbering all the while in their native tongue, which could have been, we guessed, Czech or Hungarian. They laughed often, and they loved their work, we could see that, and they filled truck after truck with lettuce, tomatoes, celery, squash, and all the other things that were grown there.

And then the earth was bare again, and the farmer came along with his tired old horse and plow and dug it up once more, leaving everything dark and dusty, and the winter would come along and the snow would turn it into a huge patch of white.

Charlie had turned four and was already playing with other kids on the street when Adraenne was born. It was a cold, blustery February day, and as soon as the call came from the doctor telling me I had a daughter, I rushed to the hospital. Once again it had been a cesarean, and once again Ruby had come through it nicely. Now our family had grown to two children, and that made it complete. There would be no more additions to the family.

And yet there was, in a way, because with our newborn child, whom we had named Adraenne—a combination of my mother's name, Ada, and Ruby's mother's name, Rachel—there came Aunt Lily again. She had been to see us often after Charlie had been born, and a strong attachment had formed between them. Now with a little baby girl in the family it was hard for her to tear herself away from us, and eventually she found a house nearby to rent. She and her husband became practically part of our family, and to our two children as they grew up she was their favorite aunt.

My mother had died soon after Charlie was born, so she never got to see the house in Laurelton, but for the others in my family it became a popular place to visit. After all, it was out in the country, with a farm right across the street. My brother Joe and his wife, Rose, and their child, Rita, came, as did my brother Saul, wearing his yarmulke and tzitzit, with the fringes sticking out from the top of his pants, and with him his tall, cigarette-smoking wife, Estelle, and their son, Irwin. My sister Rose came too, still wearing her haughty expression, accompanied by her good-natured, perpetually smiling husband, Jim, whom you would have seen on weekdays in the window of a restaurant on Sixth Avenue wearing a chef's white uniform and tall white hat and carving a large, juicy roast beef with deft movements of the knife.

Included in the gatherings were my kid brother, Sidney, and his wife, also named Rose, and their son, Ted. Sidney, the baby whose cries had awakened me once when I was ten years old and had stirred in me some small understanding of the mystery of birth, had grown to be a six-foot, hulking man and was a successful magazine publisher.

I had built a grape arbor over the driveway in front of the garage, and it was here in the summertime that our family gatherings took place, with bunches of grapes of all different varieties hanging over our heads, and the aromas in our nostrils. It was pleasant, and there was much laughter and there was a good deal of reminiscing about the old days in England and Chicago, and soon I would be busy with the barbecuing of steak and hot dogs, and Ruby would be cutting up the cherry pies she had baked with the sour cherries I had pulled from the cherry tree in our backyard, and the coffee was brewing, and in the meantime a bottle of whiskey was being passed around, and Rose was casting warning looks at Jim because he was helping himself too often to the bottle and a flush was coming on his face.

One time, I recall, when we had one of these gatherings, Jim suddenly disappeared. No one noticed it for a while, then Rose suddenly became aware that he was no longer sitting beside her, and she got up to look for him. We all joined in the search, and finally located Jim behind some bushes at the front of the house on his hands and knees searching for something. It turned out he had gone out there to get rid of the liquor he had consumed, and in doing so had lost his set of false teeth.

We all began looking for them and eventually found them, and learned for the first time that Jim's engaging smile displayed teeth that were not his own.

And yet it was Jim who, for the most part, watched out for Rose at our gatherings, and who cast warning looks at her when the topic Ruby and I dreaded came up: politics.

Before these gatherings took place Ruby and I consulted with each other as to how we might prevent such a topic from being discussed, knowing quite well from past experience what such a topic could lead to. There were some sharp divisions in the family, ranging from extreme right-wing conservatism to left-wing radicalism. Rose had not given up the Communist beliefs that had cost her a job in Chicago. She was still an ardent Communist, and two of my brothers, Joe and Sidney, were violently anti-Communist, while the third was concerned only with religion.

It was Aunt Lily's husband, Peo, however, who clashed most frequently with Rose. He was generally a silent man. He had been a construction worker once, a lather who was part of the process of building a plaster wall, and during this time he had been an active member of the IWW—Industrial Workers of the World—the most radical of all radical organizations. However, there had been vast changes in his life. There had been a revolution in the building industry that virtually did away with plaster walls, replacing them with drywall or Sheetrock, as it was called. Peo's trade became obsolete, and he was too old to learn a new one; as a result, he had been out of work for a number of years. To make matters worse, the IWW had fallen into decline and scarcely existed anymore, and Peo sat home most of the time smoking cigarettes. But he had lost none of his belief in the organization, and he blamed the Communist Party for its downfall. They had stolen the IWW's member-

ship, he claimed, and helped the capitalists destroy their most po-
tent enemy.

It was a charge that Rose violently disputed, and it came up at
one of the family gatherings under the grape arbor, with the two
shouting at each other. Ruby and I had been helpless to prevent the
subject of politics coming up, as it did so often among all people
with the threat of war hanging over us and the country divided over
our entry into it.

It had begun with that, and there seemed to be general agree-
ment that Hitler had to be stopped somehow; then Rose began to
praise the Soviet Union for what it was doing to battle the Nazi
armies, and this brought Sidney into the discussion, saying bitterly
that if the Communists hadn't signed their infamous pact with
Hitler before the war started there might not have been any war, and
Rose telling him angrily he didn't know what the hell he was talking
about. Now it was starting, and Ruby and I were casting worried
looks at each other. Then Peo came out of his silence to say, "Maybe
they got what they had coming to them."

Rose flashed an infuriated look at him. "Is that so?" she said. "Is
that the official word of the IWW—assuming that organization is
still alive?"

Peo's look at her was equally murderous. "If it isn't," he flashed
back, "it's because you Commies killed it."

He'd used the word *Commies,* which was the worst kind of in-
sult. So they were at it again, and there was no stopping them. They
went at it hammer and tongs, only this time it became more than
words, and when Rose accused the IWW of being a bunch of stupid
bums who couldn't read or write, Peo took the piece of cherry pie
Rose had given him before and threw it into her face. There was a
violent uproar, with Jim holding Rose back from attacking Peo, and

Aunt Lily holding Peo back, and everybody shouting, and the children looking on in fright, and Ruby and me helpless.

It wasn't long after that day that our neighbor Mrs. Birnbaum came bursting unceremoniously into our house shouting at the top of her voice, "The Japs have bombed Pearl Harbor!"

Ruby and I looked at each other. The same thought was in our minds: I would be drafted. I was physically fit. It wouldn't be long before even married men with children would be drafted, and I would be no exception. Soon enough all this took place, and to make matters still worse, word came that Ruby's brother, Morris, who had been drafted despite his mental condition, had been wounded in a battle on Saipan.

When we received the news about Morris, Ruby nearly collapsed. This was the second time I had seen her like that; the first time had been when her mother died suddenly of a heart attack four years earlier. Only this time it was worse because of the shadow that had been hanging over us and the fact that I myself might be called into the army.

I tried to reassure her. "I doubt very much if I'll be called," I said. "They rarely take married men with children."

But I was wrong. One day a letter beginning "Greetings" came, summoning me to Grand Central Station for my physical examination. I had to be there at eight in the morning. It took an hour to get there, so I was up at six, and Ruby was up with me, and she was trying to hide the way she was feeling. I had been told that if you passed the exam you were inducted immediately into one of the military forces. You did not go home. So this could be the last time I saw her and the children. It was not with pleasant feelings that I ate the breakfast Ruby made for me, and I'm sure she was repressing tears. This could be the first time in our married life that we would be separated for an extended time. The early morning light was thin and gray. I had not wanted her to turn on the light. I did not want her to see my face. She ate a little with me, then it was time to go.

I went into the kids' rooms. Both were asleep. I bent down and kissed them, and Ruby came to the door with me. I took her in my arms, perhaps for the last time, and felt her warmth against me, and when I kissed her I felt the wetness in her eyes. I turned back once as I walked from the house, heading for the bus. She was still standing there in the doorway. In the thin light her figure was shadowy, but I saw her wave to me and blow a kiss. I blew one back at her.

THE ENTIRE HUGE WAITING ROOM at Grand Central Station had been taken over by the military for the physical examinations, and it was packed with men when I arrived. Some were already standing in the line that had to pass through a battery of doctors, and they were all naked. I was directed to a room where I could take my clothes off, and then I came out and joined the line at the end, though it was not the end for long. In my hand I carried a form that listed all the various parts of the body to be examined and that would be checked off as good or bad by the examining doctors, who sat at desks in a long assembly line.

The line moved slowly, and the hours dragged on. I finally reached the first doctor. He tested my heart, my lungs, and my pulse, and he checked these off with one of the two pens he had in readiness. One had red ink, the other blue ink. If it was checked in blue, it was favorable; the red was unfavorable. For the next hour as I moved slowly from one doctor to another my chart showed all blue checks. And then came the eye doctor.

He couldn't have been much older than I was, and he didn't

seem to be in an agreeable mood. He barked, "Look at the chart and read it off to me." I had been troubled lately with watery eyes, and they were watering then, so I was having a bit of trouble reading the chart. I told this to the doctor, but he brushed it aside irritably and said, "Go on reading."

I did, stumbling my way through it, and managed to complete everything except the last line, which was in very tiny letters.

"Keep trying," he insisted.

I did, and guessed my way through haltingly. He stopped me and asked abruptly, "What kind of work do you do?"

"I'm a reader," I said.

"A what?"

I'd had trouble with this before. Who knows what a reader is? I explained to him what I did, reading books mostly for a moving picture company to determine their cinematic possibilities.

"How many books do you read in a week?" he asked.

"An average of five," I said.

He stared at me. "Five books a week?" he said with a touch of incredulity. "You've been reading five books a week? For how long?"

"I've been doing it for about seven years," I said.

His stare grew wider. He shook his head several times, then bent over my chart with a pen in his hand. The pen that he wrote with was the one with red ink.

I came finally to the end of the line. It had taken all morning and well into the afternoon to get through all the examining doctors. Now I had reached the desk where the last doctor sat. He was the judge. He read the chart, and we held our breath as he did so. There were two rubber stamps in front of him, one of which would say ACCEPTED, the other REJECTED. Which one would he use? My fate was in this man's hand.

I watched him as he studied my chart. He seemed to be at it for a long time, as if he could not make up his mind. I saw his eyes fasten on the note in red ink that the eye doctor had scribbled. And then with my heart thumping I saw his hand reach toward the two stamps. It touched one and then it touched the other. He could still not decide. Finally, his hand clasped over the one on the left. He crashed it down on the chart. In big letters it said REJECTED.

I tried not to show any expression on my face. But if one had been there, it would have shown the immense burst of relief I felt. The first thing I did was rush for a telephone, and I called Ruby.

"I've been turned down," I said. "I'm four-F."

"What does that mean?" she said in a tremulous voice.

"It means that I don't have to go into the army."

I heard her give a great sigh.

I knew she felt the same way I did. There is nothing heroic about this, but that is the way I felt.

Chapter Six

THE ONCOLOGIST'S OFFICE WAS CROWDED. THERE WERE NO MORE seats available in the waiting room, and some had to stand. We were lucky. We had come early enough to get three seats together. Adraenne had come, of course. She had taken time off from the hospital to be with Ruby for the bone marrow test, and even though the doctor with whom she worked had objected strenuously, nothing could have kept her away.

Our elation over the rise in Ruby's hemoglobin count had been short-lived. It had taken a sudden, dramatic drop, and not only that, but the platelet count had dropped too, and that was always a danger sign. A bone marrow test would determine just what was going on, the doctor had said. So here we were waiting our turn to see the oncologist, but all three of us were quite cheerful, with Adraenne assuring us that the test would be negative.

"And if it isn't?" I asked, too late to catch the warning look that came from Adraenne's eyes.

She resembled her mother a great deal. She was of the same height, with the same oval-shaped face and large dark eyes, except that the dark brown hair had a slightly reddish tint to it. She was quick to answer my question. "If is isn't," she said, with a carelessness to her tone that I knew was feigned, "then the worst it can mean is more Procrit. Mom has the kind of anemia that you don't have to worry about."

We didn't discuss it any more, and Ruby hardly seemed to have been listening anyway and seemed little concerned over any outcome. We were chatting over various other things not medical when Ruby's name was called by a nurse.

The two of them went in together, and I remained there waiting. It must have taken about thirty minutes before Adraenne came out alone. I could not tell from the expression on her face what the result of the test might have been.

"Where's Mom?" I asked.

"She's dressing. She'll be out soon." She sat down next to me.

"So what happened?" I said. "Did they take the test?"

"Yes."

"Then how did it go? Is everything all right?"

"Everything went fine. It wasn't an easy test to take. The doctor had to stick a large needle into her hip bone, but he knew his business and it all went quickly and Mom had very little pain."

"And you got the result?"

"Yes."

"So what is it?" I asked impatiently.

Adraenne drew closer to me. She put an arm around my shoulder and her head close to mine and said softly, "Mom has leukemia."

My heart froze. I sat still for a moment, then bent forward and put my face in my hands and cried. She held me tightly, and I recovered enough to ask, "Does she know?"

Adraenne shook her head. "No, the doctor didn't tell her. He just told me."

"Then she mustn't know," I said.

Adraenne thought for a moment. "Not yet, perhaps."

"Not anytime," I said firmly, angrily. "I don't want her to ever know."

She shushed me then, for Ruby was coming out, smiling, evidently happy that it was all over, and seeming to take it for granted that there was nothing wrong with her. My daughter and I put on a good act of believing the same thing. We went out, all three of us, in a seemingly lighthearted mood for lunch at a nearby restaurant, and as far as Ruby was concerned, it might almost have been a celebration; she knew nothing of the misery that was inside the other two of us.

But there was trouble later with Charlie. I told him of the diagnosis and our determination to keep it from his mother, and he was furious. He said it was wrong. We had no right to keep it from her. But I was just as angry. What good would it do to tell her? I wanted to know. Would it cure her leukemia? Would it make her feel better to know that she had an incurable disease and might die soon?

"Yes," he shouted. "She would reconcile herself to what is going to happen and it would give her peace of mind."

"Nonsense," I shouted back. "It would put her in a nightmare of horror with that hanging over her. She would be more peaceful not knowing. And that's the way it's going to be. You're not going to say a word to her about it."

Fortunately, Ruby was not in the house when we were discussing this. Adraenne had taken her out shopping when Charlie came from his home in Pennsylvania. When I told Adraenne about the argument later, she was silent for a moment, then said, "Perhaps Charlie was right. Mom should know. But I want to tell her myself, and there's something else I will tell her that will help a good deal. You too."

She had done a good deal of investigation with doctors and had learned of a study that was being made of cases like Ruby's at Mt. Sinai Hospital. They were experimenting with a new form of chemotherapy that had none of the side effects of that in use now, and thus far the results had been promising. The study was only open to a certain number and all the slots had already been filled, but Adraenne had pulled strings and Ruby was to be admitted.

"So you see," she said, "I'd have to tell her that she has leukemia in order to explain to her why she has to go into this study."

I no longer had any objection. It had changed the whole picture for me. I now had hope. And after Adraenne had her talk privately with her mother, I felt better yet. Ruby had taken the news calmly and with her usual intelligent understanding. Actually, she was no stranger to leukemia. Two of her cousins had died from it when they were very young. I worried that this might have had an adverse effect upon her, but on the contrary, she dismissed it lightly.

"They were just kids when they got it, not even married, and here I am, an oldie, with a full life behind me, and a good life, and a husband I love, and a marriage of many years that many other women would envy, with children and grandchildren. So I am not complaining. If I died now, I would be satisfied. I have had everything that any woman could want."

"You are not going to die now," Adraenne said, and told her about this new program at Mt. Sinai Hospital that she could go into.

It would not require her to stay in the hospital. She would have to go there once a month to be checked, but otherwise the treatments, consisting simply of injections of the chemotherapy, could be given at home, and Adraenne herself would give them. "But you don't have to do it, Mom," Adraenne said. "There is no guarantee that the injections will help, but there is a chance that they will. It's up to you."

Ruby sat quietly for a while, thinking, then said, "I'll try it. I want to live. I'll fight this thing."

So FOR A WHILE it seemed as if the nightmare was over, and we were jubilant over the results of the first few treatments. Adraenne came every week to give them. It required the mixing of two different chemicals to make the solution that she injected, a process too complicated for even Blake to have handled, and certainly not me.

In addition, in order to maintain the proper blood count, Ruby had to receive blood and platelet transfusions at the local hospital, sometimes as often as twice a week. I would always go with her and sit beside her bed while the blood or the platelets would drip slowly into her arm. She would lie back comfortably and read a book or magazine, and I would read too. It would take several hours and a pleasant, smiling nurse would bring us both lunch, and we would chat as we ate. This was how we spent a good part of the months that were left to us, and I would sometimes hold her hand and we would look at each other and smile, as if this whole thing were just another one of those excursions we used to take together in strange places in various parts of the country, enjoying it all mostly because we were together.

I loved her then as much as I had before, and perhaps even more because of the threat that was hanging over her and her helplessness lying there, with the slow steady drip of the blood into her body the only protection against losing her completely. And yet, coming out of the hospital after each transfusion, she was in a joyous mood, refreshed and strengthened, as if, she once told me, she had drunk a gallon of wine.

For a short while more we were a happy couple again, enjoying our walks around the lake, holding hands like a newly married couple, as one admiring neighbor told us. And always Ruby found strength to give her yoga lesson at the clubhouse. Every Wednesday morning we would be up early, and as Ruby put on her leotard I would watch her and marvel at her figure and its youthfulness, which she had retained into her nineties, and I would have to restrain myself from going up to her and taking her in my arms.

Then there was that last time when I drove her to the clubhouse and picked her up and she looked tired, so tired that I was worried and called Adraenne.

She was at work then, at the hospital, but she left immediately and rushed right over to us. She took Ruby's temperature. To our relief, it was just a bit above normal. A high temperature could have indicated an infection, and Dr. Silverman, in charge of the study, had warned that in her condition she would have great difficulty fighting off an infection.

Adraenne stayed over with us that night, despite the fact that she had to be at the hospital early the next day. She could barely make it if she took an eight o'clock bus to New York, and that meant getting up not later than seven. But we were awakened even earlier than that by Ruby. She was not feeling well. Once more Adraenne took her temperature, and this time it was 102 degrees, well above normal.

Alarmed, Adraenne called Dr. Silverman. He instructed her to bring Ruby into the hospital immediately. We called Charlie, getting him out of bed. He lived in Pennsylvania, more than an hour's drive away, but he made it in less time than that. Ruby didn't want to go to the hospital. I remember how she looked up at me as she lay in the bed, her eyes begging me not to take her away, and said in a whisper, "I have a premonition."

I was angry. "Nonsense," I said. "You have to go. There's absolutely nothing to be afraid of. You'll probably only have to be there a day or two until your temperature goes down, and then you'll be home again."

I think often of that morning, of the gray light creeping into the room, and of Ruby there in the bed and looking up at me with that imploring look in her eyes. Had I done the right thing? Would it not have been better to let her stay home and to heed what she was saying? Was there such a thing as a premonition? And why did I have to be so angry with her?

Adraenne and I have talked this over, because we were both conscience-stricken later, but Adraenne has convinced me that what we did was right. Otherwise there would have been no chance at all, and we would not have had the doctors and the equipment and medications that were necessary in the battle that took place to fight the infection that had occurred.

It took ten long agonizing days. I don't know how many doctors came in to see Ruby, to bend over her, to touch her here and there, to ask her where the pain was, which she could never answer coherently. We had a private nurse for her day and night. Nevertheless, Adraenne and I took turns staying with her nights. They had put a cot in the room for us, and we took turns sleeping there. When it was my night off I would go to Adraenne's apartment in Brooklyn Heights to sleep, and then I'd come back early to relieve her so that she could go to work.

For a while, for just one little while, it seemed as if the battle had been won. A miracle had taken place. Her temperature dropped to near normal. Doctors clustered around her, amazed. Ruby was smiling. I bent down to her, jubilant, and said, "Darling, how would you like to go home?"

She looked up at me with hope and wonder in her eyes and said, "Oh, yes, yes, yes. When?"

"Perhaps even tomorrow," I said.

I was quite serious. I believed then that such a thing was possible. Charlie was there, ready to drive her home. The doctors thought perhaps we should wait a bit longer. And then by nightfall it started to go the other way and our hopes were dashed. The pains had come back, the temperature had risen.

It was a different kind of infection, a new kind in the colon, and they let us know there were no drugs for it. Only an operation on the colon could save her, and an operation was out of the question. Ruby knew little of what was happening. She was in constant pain, and they began giving her morphine, and she slipped in and out of consciousness. I sat there beside her bed holding her hand, barely conscious myself, dazed and not believing what was happening.

Once, during this time, I heard Adraenne talking to the doctor she worked for over the phone. She had stopped going to work entirely and was in the room with Ruby day and night, and now she was trying to explain it to him.

"I can't come," she was saying, keeping her voice down even though Ruby was in her drugged sleep. "My mother is dying."

I could not hear his voice, but Adraenne told me later that he said, "I have my practice to think of."

"I have my mother to think of," Adraenne said, and hung up. Afterward, after this was all over and she was able to go back to work, the pressure continued, and she had to resign.

Occasionally, for a brief period, Ruby would awaken, and there was some recognition in her eyes as she looked at me. I was holding her hand and bending close to her, and she whispered something to me. It was barely audible but I heard it.

"Darling," she whispered, "don't forget to take your vitamin pills in the morning."

"I won't," I promised, and forced myself to keep her from knowing I was crying.

These were the last words we would ever speak to each other. She did not come awake again. Adraenne and I both spent that night in the room with her, taking turns during the night to lie down on the cot. The morphine dosage had been increased, and Ruby was in a heavy sleep, her breathing noisy. Both Adraenne and I were awake when dawn came. It was a gray September morning and I went to the window and looked out. Curiously, the hospital overlooked Central Park. I could see the trees and bushes beginning to emerge out of the shadows, and I remembered how much this place had meant to us, and how important a part it had played in our life together.

I was thinking of that when suddenly Adraenne let out a cry. "Dad, she's stopped breathing. She's dead!"

I swung around, shocked and disbelieving, and then I rushed to the bed. There she was, lying very still and white, and I kneeled down and took her in my arms and kissed her and held her.

I was crying hard and didn't want to let go of her when the doctor and nurse came into the room. But they finally made me go out when they came for her with a stretcher. I went into the corridor and stood with Adraenne at my side, both of us crying. Charlie had arrived, and the three of us watched through our tears as they wheeled her out of the room, her body covered with a white sheet. They went past us and down the hallway to the elevator. There was a pause while they waited for the elevator to come. Then the door slid open and they wheeled the stretcher into it, and the door closed, and that was the last I saw of her.

Chapter Seven

1950

WHEN WORLD WAR II ENDED, BIG CHANGES TOOK PLACE IN THE country, and these changes affected my life as well as many others. The most noticeable change was in the rooftops of houses and apartment buildings. Suddenly, they began to sprout forests of what might have been modern metal sculptures but were actually antennae for the newfangled television. People were buying sets all over the country, and as a result, movie theaters were practically deserted.

For the first time in its existence, the movie industry was hard hit. Audiences were staying home glued to this new magic form of entertainment, and it was because of this that my long career as a reader came to an end. I walked into the story office at RKO, the company I had been working for during the last four years, and found everyone in mourning. Word had come from Hollywood that the office was to be closed. Everybody was to be let go, from the editor on down. I was out of a job for the first time in many years.

Only this time I was forty years old. I had two children to support and soon to be put through college. We had taken another mortgage on the house, after the first one had been paid off, to help with mounting expenses. Who would hire me now? There were no more reading jobs. I went from one studio to another. They were all waiting for orders to close up. It looked very much as if the movie industry were a thing of the past. What in hell was I going to do?

"You can write," Ruby said to me when I told her the situation. She was as sympathetic and understanding as she had always been, and comforting, and with no less faith in my writing ability than ever. "You'll earn some money from your writing, and if you don't, we'll manage. Just don't worry."

She was right about our being able to manage. She also confessed to me later that she considered what had happened a blessing, as now I could write my own things instead of reading what others had written.

We were not broke. We had managed to save money, and a short time before this Ruby had left her federal job to become a school secretary at a much higher salary.

Just the same, I struggled hard to make my own contribution. I did not want it to be a repeat of the time when we were first married and I was out of work for months. I wrote, but not a novel this time. I wrote potboilers to make quick money, articles for *Popular Mechanics* and the Sunday supplements of newspapers. "What Men Won't Do for a Thrill" was one of my masterpieces; "A Day in the Life of a Strip Tease Artist" was another that I did for *American Weekly,* the Hearst papers' Sunday supplement. I even wrote scripts for comic magazines, and that made money for me also. But it was a toothache that brought me the bonanza I never expected.

Sitting in the dentist's office waiting my turn, I took a magazine off the rack to read. It was called *Your Dream Home,* and it was the thinnest magazine I had ever seen. The front cover featured a picture of a modern ranch house with a builder's name underneath, and on the back cover were the magazine's only advertisers, their names and addresses enclosed in uniform rectangles, and all apparently were subcontractors.

The whole thing puzzled me. What the hell kind of magazine was this? Or was it simply a mailing piece to promote the services of the builder on the front cover? I looked for the masthead. There was none, but in tiny print at the bottom of a page was a publisher's name and an address in northern New Jersey. I tore it out and put it in my pocket just as the dentist's nurse came out for me.

Regardless of what kind of magazine it was, it looked like an easy market for me. The articles I read in its eight pages were badly written, and I knew I could do better. I wrote one on the beauty and durability of maple furniture and sent it in to them. The reply came much sooner than I had expected, and it was in the form of a telephone call.

A man's deep, gravelly voice spoke to me, introducing himself as Myron Hallerman, publisher of *Your Dream Home,* saying he'd read my article and had been impressed with it. He was sending me a check for a hundred dollars, and would I care to have lunch with him and discuss the possibility of doing further work for his magazine?

I was stunned. A hundred bucks! It was three times what any of the bigger magazines had paid me. And would I have lunch with him? Yes, I said, and did everything I could to keep my voice steady.

Fortunately, we had a car then, a 1950 Studebaker Champion that we had treated ourselves to before the collapse of the movie industry, and I was able to drive out to New Jersey. I was in for a surprise. Considering the skinny little bit of a magazine that I had become involved with, I expected a cubbyhole of an office. Instead, it occupied an entire floor at the top of a five-story office building. And there were quite a number of girls bent over typewriters clattering away, a receptionist, everything.

Myron Hallerman's private office was large and impressive, with paneled walls, a comfortable black leather sofa and chairs, and an enormous glass-topped mahogany desk behind which he sat in a high-backed carved chair that was like a throne. He was a big man, about my age, heavyset, with an aggressive, rather swarthy face and a hand outstretched to welcome me. "Glad you could come. Sit down. Have a drink?"

There was a liquor cabinet behind him—well stocked, I would discover later. But that time I shook my head and said, "No, thanks. It's a bit too early for me."

It wasn't for him, but he didn't drink that time. We chatted for a while, I telling him about myself, my wife and children, my job as a reader for fifteen years, he telling me about himself, he too married with two children, boy and girl, which gave us something in common to start with.

We hit it off at the start, but even more so in the restaurant, where he seemed to be well known. We were seated in a booth and well tended by an attractive young waitress who smiled a lot at him and didn't mind when he patted her buttocks. I had two martinis and he two Scotches before steaks were served, and we talked a lot, he telling me that he'd graduated from an ivy league school, but instead of becoming the doctor his parents wanted him to be, he'd become a salesman, selling every goddamn thing there was to sell, as he put it in the gravelly voice. He loved selling, especially when it involved the challenge of selling things that people didn't want and he was able to talk them into buying. And then finally he hit on the toughest of all things to sell: a magazine.

The postwar building boom had given him the inspiration. He'd just come back from the war with a bit of money in his pocket that he'd won at crap games, and was looking for a business of his own. He devised *Your Dream Home,* a magazine that a builder could send out to prospective home buyers to whet their appetite for a home still further and lure them into the builder's office. It would appear to be the builder's own personal magazine, with his name on the front cover and all sorts of advice inside on how to decorate and furnish the home.

"And it doesn't cost the builder a dime," Myron explained to me, leaning forward across the table and tapping my arm to emphasize this point. "Not a goddamn dime."

"Then who pays for it?" I asked, aware that he wanted me to ask this question.

"The guys on the back cover," Myron said, grinning a little. "They're his subcontractors, and they'd better come across or else they can look for work elsewhere. Although," he added, perhaps seeing me wince, "they get their money's worth in the business the magazine brings. And it only costs 'em ten dollars a month for the ad, which is peanuts compared to what they get back. It works for everybody, including me, of course."

"How many of these builders do you have?" I asked.

"It started out with one a year ago," Myron said. "I ran around the country selling my head off before I got that one, and then it took off like a rocket, and I've quit selling myself and I've got two dozen salesmen doing it for me in every part of this goddamn country. We're up to six hundred services—that's what we call 'em, services—a month, each one bringing in an average of two hundred dollars."

I did some mental arithmetic, and whistled inwardly. Two hundred a month times six hundred came to over $1.4 million a year; there were thousands more builders to sell to, and the business was only a year old. I stared at him, and he laughed back at me. He knew what I was thinking. Then he became serious. He leaned forward and tapped my hand again.

"This is where you come in," he said. "Editorially, I've not been doing as well as at sales. I've been relying mostly on freelancers, and they all stink. I need a bit more class in the writing to get this magazine to where I want it to go. And that's the top. I can beat Henry Luce, Hearst, any of 'em. But first I've got to get myself an editor who can turn a rag into riches, and I think you're the man for it. I knew that the minute I read that article of yours. It had the class I was looking for. Would you be interested?"

It took me several moments to collect myself. This was more than I had expected, much more. I was being offered a job. "But I've never edited a magazine before," I found myself saying.

"That's all right," he said. "I've never published a magazine before and I'm doing all right."

We both laughed. He ordered another drink for me. The steaks had come. We ate heartily, I more from excitement than hunger. We chatted some more.

"How would a hundred a week be to start?" he asked. "And you can be your own man. Come when you want, go when you want. No nine to five."

A hundred a week! I'd been making thirty-five a week tops as a reader. The steak went down inside me in lumps. I was muddled with everything—the offer, the martinis, the sudden, swift change in my life. I think I said something. I'm not sure.

I DROVE HOME in a daze. Just the same, I managed to keep my eyes on the road and drive slowly since I had a lot to live for now. Through my muddled mind I went over the offer I'd been made. My conscience was troubling me. I wasn't sure how ethical this business was. Were these subcontractors being blackmailed into advertising? Did I want to get mixed up with this sort of thing?

Then I began to think of Ruby, and how long I'd burdened her with my lack of money, and the lean contributions I had made to the upkeep of the home when I did have a job of sorts. Wasn't it time I brought her some good news for a change and pitched in with some real money? This was my chance.

It tipped the scales in favor of pushing my scruples aside and telling her only what I wanted her to hear and keeping the rest to myself. And it was well worth it when I saw her face light up and her eyes widen when she heard the salary I'd been offered. Like me, she had expected the meeting to be simply to arrange for more freelance work. But this came as a delightful surprise.

She threw her arms around my neck and kissed me. "I knew somebody would recognize your talents sooner or later," she said.

"It's kind of later," I said a bit grimly.

"No, it isn't," she said. "You're still my strong, young, handsome hero. And lover," she added.

"That part I like," I said, and kissed her. Now, having thought it all over, I believe she would have said the same thing if there had been no job, no hundred a week.

We were both pretty happy that day, but just the same I kept my fingers crossed about that job and about Myron Hallerman himself.

I WOULD BE with Myron Hallerman for the next twenty years, and during that time, the publishing company grew to six magazines, not all in the building field and not all as successful as *Your Dream Home,* but moneymakers enough to enable Myron to erect his own building in New Jersey, where he also lived, and to put in his own printing plant.

I was editor in chief with a private office, a private secretary, an assistant editor, an artist, steady increases in salary, and a bonus at Christmas. Yes, sir, I was doing great. But I was paying a price for it. I had discovered almost immediately that Myron Hallerman needed more than an editor. He needed a confidant, a pal, and I was it. He thought nothing of interrupting my work and calling me into his office so that he could unburden himself of his troubles, of which he had plenty.

If it was not the salesmen who were giving him headaches, with their eternal requests for advances on commissions or money to fix a broken car or to bail them out of jail for drunk driving, then it was his wife, and she gave him the biggest headache.

His marriage was not like mine. I gathered that as I listened to him during those sessions in his office when he called me in to chat and perhaps have a drink, and he poured out all his troubles along with the liquor—sometimes at ten in the morning, and perhaps when he'd just come in after a quarrel with his wife. She was a neurotic woman and gave him no peace in the house; the office was no escape from her either because she came in quite often. She was a tall, thin woman with haggard features that had long since lost what attractiveness they might have once had. She would barge right into Myron's office regardless of how busy he might be, and though the door was closed, the entire office would soon hear them quarreling.

She was a wild spender of money, Myron told me, even though she had come from a poor family where every nickel counted. She was forever refurnishing the house. No sooner had they bought new furniture than she tired of it and decided to redo the house again. And now she was tired of the house itself and was after him to build another one, this time according to her specifications, which would cost a fortune. They quarreled often, and sometimes when they did, she went out to a jewelry store and bought some expensive diamond ring or bracelet just to spite him.

Myron was a very unhappy man despite all his success in publishing. And I felt sorry for him. But what advice could I give him? My own family was altogether different from his. My wife was absolutely perfect, at least in my eyes. What could I say to him? I simply listened and sympathized.

Perhaps that was all he wanted—someone to listen, someone to whom he could pour out all the things that were tearing him apart.

Chapter Eight

2002

I CANNOT REMEMBER MUCH OF WHAT HAPPENED AFTER RUBY DIED. Everything seemed vague and shadowy. I was conscious of people around me, voices whispering, almost like a dream. They were my children and grandchildren, the grandchildren grown up now, the five of them who had once played so happily around our golden willow tree now adults, some still in college, some working and on their own. They had all come to see Ruby while she was in the hospital during those last few days. They had loved her too, and they were still here now to be with me—not in my house, but in Adraenne's apartment in Brooklyn Heights or Charlie's house in Pennsylvania. They did not want me to go home yet and be alone there.

But sooner or later I would have to face the emptiness of the house without her. I knew that as I began to emerge from the fog I was in, and those terrible moments of realizing that she was no longer alive, and the uncontrollable fits of weeping. They were afraid of my being alone and wanted me to stay longer, but although I dreaded it, I felt a strong urge to be back there and be by myself, however terrible an ordeal it would be.

I said good-bye to all of them. Charlie drove me home. He wanted to come in and stay with me for a while, but I told him no, I would rather be by myself. I waited until he had gone, and then unlocked the door and stepped inside. I closed the door behind me and stood still for a moment in the deep silence of the house. My eyes went around the living room, and they fell on the book that was open on the large coffee table next to the couch. I remembered that she had sat there reading on the last night she was here, and the book was open at the page where she had left off.

A lump came into my throat as I saw it. I knew the book. It was one of Doctorow's, a favorite author of ours. She'd had difficulty tearing herself away from it that night. I stood for a while longer, afraid to venture farther into the house. My eyes swung around. Everything I saw reminded me of her: the chairs, the tables, the paintings on the walls, things we had bought together, the good times we'd had buying them. I began to wander through the house, going from room to room and seeing the things that reminded me of her.

In the kitchen I saw her apron draped over the back of a chair. She had been in a hurry to get to her book and had forgotten to hang it up. In the bathroom was her toothbrush, the dental floss beside it on the shelf over the sink, and I remembered how diligently she would floss her teeth after every meal.

The bedroom was hard to take. The bed was still unmade, everything the way we had left it that morning when we had hurried her to the hospital. I stood there for a long time looking at it, thinking.

I was ninety-two years old. How much longer could I possibly live? Even the most optimistic of statistics would have said not much longer. Perhaps it could be any day. So what would be lost if I hastened it just a little? Even if I did not believe in a hereafter, a life after death, I would no longer have to suffer the misery of being without her.

Such was my reasoning, and with the deepening of winter, the bitterly cold weather that kept me locked in the house for days at a time, and the loneliness, my depression grew, and I kept thinking of the ways and means by which people took their own lives, and what method I could use for myself.

I brooded over it constantly, and finally decided to get some information from my daughter, putting it to her obliquely. A nurse practitioner, she worked in a hospital that specialized in cancer and where deaths were frequent. She came to see me regularly every two weeks, making sure that I was being properly cared for, and preparing enough meals to last for a few days.

On one of these visits I asked her, trying to sound casual and merely curious, if there were not ways doctors used to end the suffering of a patient and speed up the process of dying. She was not fooled. She did not answer my question, but took hold of my hand, looked directly into my eyes, and said something that I would not forget.

"Dad, you have lost a wife you loved very much, but we have lost a mother we loved just as much. You are all we have left, and we need you now more than we ever did."

It struck home. Not until then did I realize that they were going through the same suffering I was, and it awakened me to the sense of responsibility that I'd always had toward my son and daughter from the day they were born.

It drove away all thought of suicide. It did not end my grief; that might never totally happen. But it gave me a reason to want to go on living, no matter how little time there was left for me, and to be able to function in a more normal fashion. In order to do that, I needed help, and I turned to what had been offered me before but which I had refused.

In the hospital there had been a palliative group that went among dying patients and offered counsel and comfort to the relatives gathered around the bedside. They came into Ruby's room one morning while Adraenne and I were there and Ruby lay in a morphine-drugged sleep, breathing heavily. We were puzzled at first, not knowing who they were. There were three of them, and they introduced themselves, the man a doctor, one of the two women a nurse practitioner, the other woman a social worker specializing in bereavement.

As soon as we learned who they were and what their purpose was, we wanted none of them. We were both resentful and angry, both still clinging to the belief that Ruby was not dying and would recover.

They were patient with us and tried gently to convince us that this was the end for her. The doctor stood looking down at her and said, "What you are witnessing right now is the soul leaving the body. . . ."

I was abrupt with them and made it clear that I did not agree with him and was not interested in his services. In fact, I was furious. I turned my back on him and they left. Now, thinking about it, I wished I had not behaved in that fashion, and perhaps I could have benefited a great deal from what they had to say.

But there were several similar groups in the area where I lived, which had plenty of retirement communities where deaths took place often among the elderly residents. I chose one group that met at a local hospital. There were about twenty people, mostly women, seated around a long conference table in the meeting room, all having suffered the loss of a loved one, and all, I would soon discover, going through pretty much what I was going through. A young social worker by the name of Melissa directed the meeting, and opened it with a brief talk on grief.

"What is grief?" She spoke softly, glancing around at each one as she did so. I did not need any definition of grief, but I listened carefully to what she had to say. Grief, she said, was a perfectly normal reaction to the death of a loved one. In some cases it was more devastating and lasted longer than in others. But in all cases, it was an agonizing ordeal.

Time was the best healer. Eventually time would dim the memories and lessen the pain. In the meantime, there were some practical steps that could be taken for the grief-stricken to find relief. Being with others helped. So did sharing your feelings with others. Nor was it wrong to laugh and have fun. Then she said something that would stick in my mind. "Perhaps the best way to express your grief," she said, "is the way that fits and feels right to you."

She asked for volunteers to give examples, and there was an instant response, all seeming eager to talk. One woman said it was her faith in God that kept her going. She prayed daily. Another, a man, said he was a trumpet player and told how he coped with his grief by going to his wife's grave every day and playing her favorite songs on his trumpet. Another, a woman, said that volunteering at the hospital where her husband died and helping sick patients gave her a feeling of comfort.

I left as soon as the meeting was over, though others stayed on for the coffee and cake and to chat with one another. I wanted to be alone to think over what I had heard. As simple as what I'd heard in the meeting had sounded to me, I realized there was much common sense to it also. And I was thinking of what way to express my grief could fit me.

There was only one answer, and it came to me immediately. There was my writing. Nothing could absorb me so completely as when I sat down at my desk to put words to paper, however badly I might write. I'd known that a long time ago. So why not now? Why was I hesitating? Perhaps it was because my writing had caused me grief of another sort. There had been nothing but one bitter disappointment after another. Did I want to get into that sort of thing again? I had practically given it up these past few years, busy enough and happy enough with Ruby not to mind or even think of past failures. It seemed that I would do well to think of something else that would fit.

But then there were the nights, and the nights had a lot to do with my decision to find the escape from the present I was seeking in writing. It had a lot to do also with what I wrote about.

Chapter Nine

1940

YES, THE KIDS WERE GROWING UP, AND ALONG WITH THAT WERE THE problems that come, I suppose, to all parents. Fortunately, we did not have to deal with the sibling rivalry that often comes when a firstborn child is displaced by a newborn member in the family. Charlie seemed to welcome the arrival of Adraenne as much as we did, and indeed, as she began to grow and mingle with other children, he assumed a watchful and protective attitude toward her and seemed always anxious about her welfare. He was the perfect big brother.

Shortly after the arrival of Adraenne, when Ruby had to go back to work, this time as a secretary in one of the local grade schools, one fortunately nearby, there was still another addition to the family in the form of Edna, our new housekeeper. We could not have made a better choice. She was a jolly, good-natured black woman.

Her laughter brightened our household, her cooking was good, and her care of the baby passed Ruby's closest inspection.

I myself remained watchful. I still read manuscripts when Edna first came to us, and my room was upstairs in the finished attic that had made our house so desirable when we first bought it. However, despite the privacy it gave me, I could still hear noises from downstairs, and one morning, shortly after Ruby had left the house and Charlie had gone to school, I heard the baby crying, and immediately I rushed down to find out what was the trouble.

For the first time I saw anger on Edna's face as she turned from the baby toward me.

"Mr. Bernstein," she said, putting her hands on her hips, "we might as well understand each other right here and now. Either I'm in charge of this child or I'm not, and if I am, I don't want you or anybody else interfering. And if you can't trust me, then I'll be packing my things and be on my way."

It was the last time I ever did that again. Edna was faultless, the best of all the housekeepers and maids we'd ever had, and there had been several before her. But she could only be with us, we soon discovered, for relatively short periods at a time. Her home was in South Carolina, where she had a husband and children—she never told us how many she had—but when she got tired of her home, she came north to make a little money and to have some fun, as she confided to us.

There was no question about the fun. She had friends in Harlem, and one of them frequently called for her at our house. He was a tall, amiable black man, and he came in a very large, fancy-looking car that he parked in front while he came calling. They were soon gone, the two of them, Edna waving a cheerful good-bye to us and grinning widely. She came back the next morning, always on time, looking a bit tired and sleepy, but as cheerful as ever.

I suppose she got tired of the fun too, eventually, and of us also, I guess, and so back she went to South Carolina. For several years she came and went, her return always welcomed by us.

During her absences Aunt Lily often pitched in to help with the children. She and her husband had rented an apartment in a house owned by friends of ours in the neighboring town of Rosedale, and it was a ten-minute walk to us, making it easy for her to come and go. Both Adraenne and Charlie grew fond of her, and for her they might have satisfied her own yearning for the children she'd always wanted but never had.

For Ruby and me, she gave us the chance to break away from the house and our responsibilities and visit friends or go places, while knowing that the kids were well taken care of. Ruby and I had almost forgotten what it was like to be alone together, so immersed had we been in all the changes that had taken place in our life. So it was good to be together again and have a taste of what it had been like when all we had to think about was ourselves and no responsibilities hung over us.

Thanks to Aunt Lily we were able to take a trip to England, to see the town where I had been born, and about which I have written in my book *The Invisible Wall*. I told how we arrived one rainy afternoon to find the street on which I had lived in the process of being torn down to make way for a public housing project. We stood under our umbrella for a while, looking through the drizzle at a deserted street, the two rows of empty houses without doors and windows, feeling depressed and disappointed. It was a Sunday, so there was no work being done, and the people I had hoped to see were no longer there, except one.

Yes, there was one, and she came running out to greet us, having recognized me from her window in the one house that was still occupied. It was Annie Green, whom I remembered so well as a young woman then, now an old woman, bent over, huddled in a shawl that covered her head and showed fringes of white hair, and a toothless mouth that shouted warm greetings.

Annie took us into her house and served us tea and biscuits and an abundance of information about the people who had once lived here and what had happened to them in all the years since I had gone away. Ruby and I came away refreshed and warmed, glad now that we had come.

A week of sightseeing in London and Paris followed, and by that time we were eager to get home and be with our kids again. Perhaps until then we had not realized how important a part of our life they had become. To be sure, we missed the lazy Sunday mornings when we could loaf in bed as long as we liked and spend all the time we wanted over breakfast with the Sunday *Times* scattered about us, the ease of not having to take care of anyone but ourselves, the untroubled days when we did not have children with their noise, their constant demands, their fevers and sore throats, and the worry over their school grades. But the pleasure we derived from seeing them grow and develop, and the love that came from them, made up for all that.

FROM THE START, we realized that our two children were almost exact opposites, two separate individuals with different characteristics and personalities. Charlie was outgoing; he made friends easily and had lots of them—too many, we often thought—and his mind was more on having fun with his friends, less on schoolwork. He was big for his age. Before he was twelve, when he was still in grade school, he towered over all his classmates.

Ruby and I collaborated on an article about him that was published in *Parents* magazine. "Big for His Age" was the title, and we told how it could be as much a disadvantage to a boy as an advantage. It could command the respect of other boys, but if he got into a fight with one who was his age but much more normal and smaller in height, he would be called a bully, and if he turned away from it, as he did sometimes for fear of hurting the other one, he would be labeled a coward. He was handy around the house for Ruby when it reached a point where he was taller than she was and she had to reach up for something on a shelf that was too high up for her; he did it for her with perfect ease. But generally, we pointed out in the article, far more was expected of him than he was capable of doing.

However, he weathered the period until his peers caught up with him in height without any bad psychological effects, and he grew into his adolescence as cheerful and outgoing as ever, with an abundance of friends that soon began to include girls, and with that he paid less attention to his schoolwork than ever.

"Charlie, did you do your homework?"

I can remember that remark coming from both Ruby and myself almost without fail every day. The reply was generally no. He was always truthful. I once thought his inability to tell a lie was due to lack of imagination, but I was being unjust to him. He was simply a straightforward, honest kid who could not lie to us, and it often brought on difficulties for him and for us. He could be on his way out, all dressed up, his long hair slicked back, on his way to a party or to some other kind of pleasure, and we'd stop him and ask the question: "Have you done your homework?"

"No," came the reply.

"Then do it." Ruby was the disciplinarian. I was inclined to be more lenient, and I would have let him go. But Ruby was firm, and there was good reason for it. She more than anyone could appreciate the value of schools. She'd had to wait until she was eleven years old before she could go to one. She'd come from Poland, where she was born, at that age, and there had been no schools for poor people in Poland. So, at eleven in the United States, she had to catch up with her own age group, together with learning the English language, a tremendous job, and yet she did it in one year. Now she spoke English without any trace of an accent.

She reminded Charlie of all that, and so did I, but despite our efforts to get him to follow in her footsteps, he could not work up any enthusiasm for school. His grades were low. He was bright, the teachers assured us, but he couldn't seem to pay any attention to the classwork. And then he stopped going to school at all. We knew nothing about this for a week before we received a telephone call from the principal telling us he'd been absent all that week.

He didn't deny it. He was George Washington again—he couldn't tell a lie—and we were at our wits' end as to how to handle the situation. Grounding him or taking his bike away were stopgaps, not a solution. There was counseling. We tried that, hiring a college student who was majoring in psychology, a pleasant young fellow who we thought might also serve as a role model for our son, something I should have been myself but obviously wasn't.

His name was Jud and he came twice a week in the afternoon, and he and Charlie would go upstairs to the finished attic that had become Charlie's bedroom in addition to being my office. I left the room when they came and transferred my work to the basement, which I had finished off and turned into a playroom. It seemed to be working out quite well. Charlie came out of the one-hour sessions with Jud looking quite pleased, and he seemed to have benefited from the counseling. His work at school improved a little. Ruby and I were quite pleased. Then one afternoon, after the session had begun, I found it necessary to go upstairs in order to get something there I needed. I went up the stairs quietly so that I shouldn't disturb them, and suddenly heard giggling. Puzzled, I tiptoed the rest of the way up. The door was partly open and I peeked in. They were both sprawled on the floor side by side chuckling over a comic magazine.

So this was the psychological counseling my son had been getting for the past few weeks. I'd been paying good money to have him read comic magazines.

I burst in on them shouting, "What the hell's going on here?"

Charlie looked as if he wished he could drop through the floor and disappear. Jud, however, took it quite calmly and said comic magazines were part of the method that he'd been taught at City College.

And I said, "You're full of it. Now get the hell out of here."

"Do you mind giving me my pay first?" he asked calmly.

"I do mind," I said, but I gave it to him anyway.

He left, and that was the end of the counseling.

Looking back now, I wonder if perhaps Jud was right and comic magazines were the best medicine for what ailed Charlie. Either that or simply time and patience were the only things that could solve his problem and the many other problems that assail children while they are growing up.

With Adraenne, it was another matter, and altogether different from the problems we had with Charlie. She could not get enough of school. She was at the top of her classes, and soon had skipped two grades, so she was sixteen when she graduated from high school and entered college.

She was the opposite of Charlie in other ways too. She was shy and introspective, and she could spend hours alone in her room reading or writing poetry. She did not go to parties very much, and she was very select in the friends she chose. Nor did she have boyfriends calling on her, though she was pretty from the time she was a child.

Charlie could not wait to become a Boy Scout. He wore his uniform proudly, he worked hard to get his merit badges, and he was happy when he went off to Boy Scout camp for two weeks in the summer. But Adraenne, on the other hand, resisted becoming a Brownie, and only agreed reluctantly after much urging on our part because we thought Brownies and then Girl Scouts later would serve to bring her out of her shell a little.

After considerable persuasion, we talked her into going to a Brownie camp for a week. We saw her off at the bus packed with eager, excited young girls, all anxious to get to the camp except Adraenne, who clung to us tearfully until the last moment, and Ruby and I turned away feeling sad but certain we had done our duty in forcing her to go.

Two days later came a telephone call from her. She was weeping. Could we come and get her? Immediately, I raced down there in the car, and she was waiting for me and practically flew into my arms.

So we let her drop out of the Brownies and take piano lessons instead, and she was happy with that. We invested in a baby grand that took up half the living room. It was not new, and one leg needed a bit of fixing and it was badly out of tune, but these matters were soon taken care of and Mrs. Daly came into our lives. She was the piano teacher, a solidly built woman of around forty with a breezy manner who came bursting into our house every Saturday morning to give Adraenne her lesson, and for an hour commanded in her loud voice, without ever illustrating with her own playing what she was instructing. I don't think we ever once heard her play the piano, and we were never sure that she knew how. But she had been teaching the children of Laurelton for years, and Adraenne emerged from several years of her instruction knowing at least how to play the Beethoven bagatelles.

Saturday was music day in our house. Every Saturday I drove Charlie into Manhattan to the Henry Street Settlement, where he was being taught to play the clarinet. We had been determined that our children should learn to play some instrument, and at first with Charlie it had been the violin, chiefly because I owned one from a period in my life when I attempted to learn to play it and then, having failed, had put it away in a closet. But now I brought it out, dusted it off, and gave it to my son to carry on where I had left off.

There was an orchestra at school, and at the head of it was a poor devil of a man who not only conducted but undertook to teach the students various other instruments of which he knew little. The man was half crazed with his efforts and the results he got, and sometimes he completely lost control of himself and beat the young would-be musician over the head with whatever instrument the child happened to be playing. I know Charlie got it several times with his violin, and I had to do some repair work on the fiddle.

But without ever really learning how to play his violin, Charlie was admitted to the orchestra, and a mishap took place the first day. He should never have started to learn to play this instrument in the first place because he was left-handed, and his partner in the orchestra was on that side, and when Charlie drew his bow his left elbow went into the eye of the kid beside him, knocking his eyeglasses off and almost costing him an eye. Charlie was thrown out of the orchestra at once, and the enraged conductor sent his fiddle flying after him.

We put the fiddle away for good this time, and to this day it still resides in my closet gathering dust. It shall never be played again.

But eventually Charlie's fancy turned to the clarinet, chiefly because he had seen Benny Goodman play in a movie and was inspired to follow in his footsteps. I had no objection, even though the clarinet cost me a hundred dollars. A friend steered me to the Henry Street Settlement, where they had competent teachers for all instruments and where lessons were cheap. But we had to be there by eleven and it took an hour of driving in the car to get there. That meant I had to leave no later than ten, and on this particular Saturday morning at ten Charlie was not back yet from wherever it was he had gone on his bike. I was furious. I stood outside and looked this way and that, and Ruby did some telephoning of neighbors to find out if he was with one of them.

Finally, he came tearing down the street on his bike. He was sorry. He was always sorry, abjectly. I resisted clouting him on the head and told him to get into the car, and he did. I blame myself for what followed, though it really wasn't my fault. What happened was that I raced to get to Manhattan on time, and in my rush I went through a red light and was stopped by a cop and given a ticket.

We got to the Henry Street Settlement later than ever, but at least there was still time for the lesson, and I had to be satisfied with that.

"All right," I said roughly to Charlie. "Get going."

He was still sitting in the seat beside me, not moving. "Dad," he said, "I can't."

"What d'you mean, you can't?" I snapped. "Go on, just go."

"I can't," he repeated, still not moving.

"Why?" I shouted. "Why can't you?"

"I forgot my clarinet."

This was one of those moments that doctors warn you about, when your blood pressure soars, potentially causing a stroke. I think I may have been very near that. However, I had gone through many trials in my life before this, and I'd learned something about control, which came in handy then. Something else came to my rescue too, after I had arrived home and told Ruby about it. Ruby also was blessed with this same thing: a sense of humor. We both had a good long laugh. But privately, without letting Charlie know.

THERE ARE MANY OCCASIONS in the process of raising children when a sense of humor is badly needed to save you from bursting a blood vessel. There was one other that I recall. Both my children, different from each other as they were, shared one thing in common, a love of animals, and Ruby and I had catered to that love, believing that the care of living creatures was an important part of a child's upbringing. It was fortunate that we had a house large enough for both animals and humans because in those early years of their childhood it became filled with cats and dogs, mostly homeless ones that the children's soft hearts had led them to pick up and bring home. But there were also parakeets, canaries, turtles, hamsters, and chickens. Yes, chickens. I fenced off a portion of the backyard for them, and we had a mini chicken farm that brought many objections from neighbors.

Hamsters were their latest craze. Charlie, who was generally in charge of the family pets, had decided he wanted to raise them and sell them to people, so we had a male hamster and a female hamster in one cage. There was either a lack of love between the two hamsters or a lack of knowledge about breeding because the match failed. And still Charlie, with Adraenne always going along with him, wanted a family of baby hamsters to raise, and it so happened that his birthday came along at this time and he asked that for a present we buy him a pregnant hamster.

How could we refuse? But where could we find a pregnant hamster? I went from pet store to pet store asking for one, but to no avail. I refused to give up. I had promised him I would get him a pregnant hamster, and I was determined to keep that promise. I called pet stores miles away and asked, and at last hit the right one. They had a pregnant hamster. It was far away in Pennsylvania. I drove out there and bought it; there was no doubt of its being pregnant. It was big and fat. The proprietor put it in a box for me and I put the box in the back seat of my car; I remember feeling elated, as if I'd struck gold.

I'd be just in time. Charlie's birthday was the following day. Meanwhile, the hamster would be safe in the back of the car. Just to be sure, however, I went to look. The box was empty. I was stunned. I looked around the entire car. There was no hamster anywhere. I looked under the seats, even in the glove compartment, but no hamster. How could it possibly have escaped, first from the box in which the pet store owner had put it, then from a locked car?

It was a good thing I gave a last despairing glance around, for I glanced upward and saw movement in the lining that covered the inside of the roof. Quite distinctly, there was a lump of some sort, and it was moving very slowly. I reached up with a hand and felt it. There was warmth and no longer any doubt in my mind that this was the pregnant hamster. How it had escaped from the box and how it had found its way up there will always remain a mystery, but the next important question was how to get it out of there.

I realized at once that I could never do it myself, and there was only one place I could take it to get it out: the dealer. I hesitated, and for good reason. I had bought the car only recently but had been back to the dealer with it numerous times and for various reasons, most of which I am sure the dealer considered the imagination of a neurotic customer. They were perfectly justifiable complaints to me—a squeak here, a squeak there, a strange noise in the engine, a stiffness in the steering wheel, a funny sound in one wheel. I was determined to have every little thing satisfied before the warranty ran out. But now I had to go back to him with an entirely new complaint: a hamster stuck in the roof of the car. Little wonder that I hesitated.

But it was the only way I could get that hamster out of there and to my son for his birthday. And what if it gave birth while it was still stuck up there? The horror of this frightful possibility overcame all the hesitation and embarrassment I might have felt.

I think they had seen me come so often with my car to the place where I'd bought it that the dealer had posted a lookout to warn him because several of the last times I had been there he'd been out of his office and not to be found. But a few weeks had passed since the last time and I caught him unawares. He gaped up at me from his desk as I marched into his office.

"What now?" he managed to say.

"I'm sorry," I apologized, "but I'm afraid I've got another problem with the car."

"What sort of problem?" he asked, looking as if he was about to duck out anyway.

"I've got a hamster stuck in the roof of the car, and it looks as if you're going to have to take the lining out to get to it."

For a moment he didn't say anything. He simply gazed up at me with his mouth open. He was a rather short, fat man with a thick, fleshy face; his wide mouth was open, showing a row of glistening white teeth that were obviously not his own, although that has nothing to do with my story. He finally spoke in a sort of strangled voice: "Will you say that again?"

I repeated what I had said, suddenly conscious of the fact that he might not even know what a hamster was. He didn't, and I explained it to him and went on further to add that it was pregnant and might give birth to its young ones, and since hamsters could have as many as a dozen at one time they'd be all over the car in various tight places. But I had only worsened things.

He took all of this in with a hand clapped to his forehead and a despairing look on his face, and then he called for his head serviceman. I knew him, just as he knew me. His name was Shawn. He was Irish. He was tall and lanky with very black hair, and he had a temper. We'd had a lot of arguments before this, and as he came into the office, chewing tobacco as he always did, his eyes told me what he thought of me.

"Shawn," the dealer said, "guess what the trouble is now?"

Shawn shifted the wad inside his mouth from one side to the other and bent his head a little, as if looking for a place to spit. "I'll bet he's got a rattle in the glove compartment," he said.

They must have done plenty of talking about me. I tried to smile, but I wished I hadn't come.

"You mean a rattlesnake," the dealer said. "No, it isn't that. It's something in the roof of his car. A hamster."

"A what?" The mouth opened and tobacco juice dribbled out onto his chin. He wiped it with the back of a hand that was blackened with oil, leaving a dirt mark on the chin. "What did you say?"

The dealer repeated it and went on. "It's pregnant too, and we've got to get it out fast before it gives birth and scatters its kids all over the car, maybe in the engine."

Then Shawn did something I had never seen him do before. He laughed. It was roaring laughter, with him bent over, and the wad of tobacco came out onto the floor. He picked it up and threw it into the wastebasket, still convulsed with laughter.

There's no need to go any further with the story. They took care of it, and I waited while they did it, and this time it was not covered by the warranty and I could not argue that part of it. I winced when I got the bill. It was heavy, and I think it made up for all the other jobs they'd had to do for me without payment. But the worst part came when they found the hamster and brought it to me. It was no longer moving. It was dead.

I think for a moment I had some wild thought of taking the corpse to a vet and having him open the creature with the possibility that the young hamsters might be alive. But by that time I was sick of hamsters and I let them dump it into a waste bin.

It was hard breaking the news to the kids the next day. Adraenne took it nicely, but Charlie was wild with disappointment and frustration and wept bitterly until I gave him the gift I had bought for him in place of the hamster. It was an electric train set and it made up for his great loss, but not completely, and it never would. I think he still mourns the loss of that pregnant hamster to this day, and right now he's well into his sixties and has five children of his own. He also has a dog and two cats and has lost none of his love for living things.

Chapter Ten

NIGHTS ARE SUPPOSED TO BE FOR SLEEP OR REST OR FOR MAKING love, but for me in those days after Ruby died they were endless nights of torture that seemed never to be over. I would lie awake staring up in the darkness, my mind active and my thoughts driving from one thing to another, mostly about Ruby and the time we'd spent together, and the things we'd talked about and the places we'd gone to. And all the time I was conscious of the emptiness of the bed beside me: When I stretched out my arm onto the pillow her head was not there, nor was there the warmth of her body.

Even getting into bed was a misery, not finding her there, the bed cold and empty. I could not stop thinking of her and wanting her. One night, though, I must have managed to doze off to sleep, and suddenly I heard her voice.

"Harry!"

It came to me clearly and distinctly, and I was convinced it had not been in my sleep. I shot up in bed and listened. There was nothing but that ringing silence throughout the house. I was so sure, however, that I had heard her voice cry out that I got out of bed and began to prowl through the rooms looking for her. I did not turn on lights. I went from room to room searching through the darkness, groping my way like a sleepwalker, although I knew I was fully awake.

Once, I remember, I called out to her questioningly: "Ruby?" I paused to listen. There was no answer, and I went back to bed, still quite sure that I had not been dreaming when I heard her voice.

It troubled me for days afterward, and I began to wonder if I was losing my mind. I worried over it, and I thought of it when I lay awake at night in bed. I did not believe in a hereafter. I did not believe that Ruby was up there in heaven, smiling down at me, waiting for me to join her, as some people had said in trying to comfort me for my loss of her. Then what was it that made me feel even days later that I had heard her voice?

I could not in any way account for it, nor did the voice ever come again, but out of it came the realization that if I did not do something soon to occupy my mind with some useful purpose, I might lose that mind. And once again came the thought of going back to my writing. But write what? I racked my brain for a subject that would interest me—and other people too, should I decide to try to get it published.

Lying there awake at night, with my thoughts flitting back and forth at random with no particular sequence—an event here, an event there, a place we had been to, people we had met, all racing through my mind helter-skelter, like a film that had lost control in the projector—I found myself thinking at a calmer pace of my childhood in England. The pictures were quite clear, particularly the street on which I had lived with its two rows of sad-looking brick houses facing each other across the cobblestones, with their slanted slate roofs and short, stubby chimneys sticking up into gray skies with smoke curling out of them.

Why I should suddenly have gone back to that distant point in my life is perfectly clear to me now that I think of it. I was seeking to get away as far as possible from the present with all its misery. I was looking back at a time and place where there had been enough misery in its own right but which had nevertheless been home to me, with my mother alive, and my brothers and sisters too, and friends, lots of them.

There had been poverty to battle, but something else that was just as bad if not worse, and that was bigotry, for the street was divided into two enemy camps. On one side, on my side, lived the Jews, and on the other were the Christians, and in between them was an invisible wall that kept the two sides from crossing over to each other.

Yes, I began to think of that, and the film slowed down and everything was clear, and I remembered among many things the dark, sullen, perpetually embittered figure of my father, and the times he came home drunk from the pub at night, the roar of his voice disturbing our sleep, waking us all up with a feeling of terror, and how I used to pull the covers over my head to shut out the sounds.

I thought of my mother a great deal, and how she used to struggle to keep us alive because my father, who worked as a tailor and made little money, gave her even less of it to feed us and used the rest of it for his drink and gambling. I remembered how one Saturday he'd doled out the pittance he gave her and then had gone striding

off to his pub, and she looked at the bit of money he'd thrust grudg-
ingly into her hand. With a sudden resolve she put on her hat and
coat and took me with her to the market. There I watched, frightened, as she crawled under one of the fruit stands and came out with
her two straw bags filled with half-rotten fruit she'd scavenged from
beneath the stall. This rotted fruit became the start of her little shop
that she made in our front room, which had never been furnished
because there was no money to buy furniture but which my mother
had promised us would someday become a parlor with a red plush
couch and chairs, a thick red plush carpet too, and even a piano.

But now it was a shop that sold faded fruits and vegetables. We
were bitter and resentful about it, and ashamed of the shop, not realizing that it would save our lives with the little bit of money that
came from it.

It all came flooding back to me, along with how World War I
had drawn the two sides of the street together. When Emily, the little telegram girl, came riding into our street perched high on her bi-
cycle and whistling a merry tune, everyone came out onto their
doorsteps with hands on their hearts and watched tensely to see
whose door she would stop at, taking out of her pouch one of those
dreaded telegrams with the black border around the envelope. And
upon seeing whose door it was—not theirs, thank God—they
would rush to comfort the poor, weeping newly widowed woman.
From both sides they came, and it would not matter whether you
were Jewish or Christian. There was only one side then.

And there was love too, tucked away on that street, hidden from
view. One of the lovers was my sister Lily, and the other was a Christian boy who lived opposite us. I was their secret messenger who carried notes from one to the other, and I learned too more of the cruel
bigotry that existed between us.

Everything was there in my mind, and perhaps it had been there for a long time, stored away inside me, ever since we had left England to come to America to seek a better life. But now it was begging to be written.

And write it I did. I plunged right into it the very next day, sitting down at my electric typewriter and tapping away at the keys. It was a long time since I had done that, before I'd entered my nineties, and I found things were not quite the same as before. My hands had stiffened. They did not fly across the keys as they had once done when I was younger. They were slow and I made a great many mistakes. Nor could I sit as long as I used to in a chair at the desk. I had to get up frequently and knead my fingers to loosen them, and to walk around a bit to get the blood flowing in my legs.

That was being ninety. But it did not stop me from writing *The Invisible Wall*. I had given it that title from the very beginning, and I saw my story then as a microcosm of all the walls that exist in the world today—some of them not as invisible as I portrayed ours, but actual brick or concrete walls that separated one country from another, or one race or religion from another. Regardless of how disturbed and angry all that made me feel, the writing of it did what I wanted it to do. It took my mind off my grief and carried me back into a world that I had once known more happily and where, in retrospect at least, I was comfortable and secure.

Chapter Eleven

SUMMERS WERE TRAVEL TIME FOR US WHEN THE CHILDREN WERE growing up. It was mostly for pleasure, and for the chance to be closer to our children than during the rest of the year, when school and work separated us for so many hours. But it was also for educational purposes. We thought the kids could benefit from seeing the places that had played such an important part in American history. And the kids loved it.

Perhaps it was for our benefit, too. Ruby and I had both come from poor families where there was no such thing as a vacation. We had never seen much of the world or the country itself outside of the towns where we had been born, Ruby in Poland, myself in England, and then later New York. So we were just as eager as the children to travel and see as much of the entire country as we could.

Generally, we began our trips in the month of July, and we packed enough clothing and other supplies to last us for a month, never knowing how long we would be gone. We had two cars then, one in which Ruby did her shopping and went to work, a small car that Chrysler had named the Lark, and a larger Buick that I drove to my job editing trade magazines. Naturally, we took the Buick, and we drove off in high spirits, with Ruby sitting beside me and Charlie and Adraenne in the backseat. On the seat with the children were the games and puzzles and books that would come in handy when they grew bored with the long stretches of driving in between destinations and began to carry on a bit in the backseat and annoy Ruby and me, particularly the one of us who was driving at the time.

We had learned to bring these supplies after long and often bitter experiences. I remember one time when we were crossing the seemingly never-ending miles and miles of Texas wasteland. The two of them got into a scuffle with much shouting and screaming accompanied by slaps. I was driving at the time, and I brought the car to a halt abruptly at the side of the road in a patch of sand.

"Get out!" I ordered the two of them. They quieted immediately and obeyed, and stood in the sand with the wind blowing hard and raising the dust into their faces. Behind us stretched miles and miles of empty, desolate land with no habitation in sight, not a single person. I pointed it out to them and said, "If I hear one more peep out of you two, I'm going to drop you off here and let you make your way to civilization on foot while Mom and I drive on."

It may not have been the best kind of way to discipline children, but it worked for me, and they were as quiet as two little mice for the rest of the trip. After that, however, we were careful to take along enough distractions to keep them occupied, and our trips were conducted for most of the time with two orderly passengers in the back-seat.

We went everywhere. Up in northern New York State we visited Fort Ticonderoga to see where the Revolutionary army had fought the British in a fierce battle, the cannons they used still there. We drove along the East Coast to Plymouth Rock to see where the Pilgrims had first landed, and down to Washington, D.C., to wander about the buildings and monuments of the capital, gazing up and down and all around, and getting so tired we could hardly wait to get into our hotel and into bed.

There was one trip we made to visit Davy Crockett's birthplace that got us into a bit of trouble. Our map led us deep into the backwoods of Tennessee. Unfortunately, we had arrived the day after a heavy rainfall. A stream we had to cross by way of a low, wooden bridge was overflowing, and the bridge was partially covered with water. I was at the wheel and hesitated about attempting to cross over it. Yet there was no other way to get to our destination other than by a long circuitous route.

I decided finally to chance it. I went very slowly. But the water kept getting deeper until I could no longer see the edges of the bridge. My passengers began to guide me, but their instructions soon became confusing.

"To the right," shouted Ruby.

"No, Dad, to the left," yelled Charlie.

Adraenne chimed in too, siding with her brother. "To the left, Dad."

I zigzagged slowly, trying to follow all the mixed instructions, and then it happened. The car suddenly slid and halted. The front wheel had gone over the edge and there we were stuck in the middle of the bridge, perhaps forever. In a panic, we yanked off our shoes and stockings, scrambled out of the dangerously tilted car, and waded back to where we'd come from, to find a group of natives watching us. Obviously this was nothing new to them. It had been going on all day long, car after car, and there was only one place we could get help, they told us, pointing to a cabin not far away in the woods. In that cabin we'd find a man who would take care of everything.

We found a heavyset man badly in need of a shave seated at a table eating his lunch. Hunched over a plate of beans, he did not glance at us as we came in, but said in a deep voice, "Be right with you."

He seemed to know already why we had come. He had been hauling cars off the bridge all day long and had been making a handsome sum of money out of it. And it happened after every rainfall. We stood with our wet feet waiting for him to eat his lunch. Soon he was done, wiped his mouth with the back of his hand, and got up from the chair.

"All right, folks," he said. "Follow me."

He hadn't asked anything. He knew it all. We followed him outside, and there was the truck he used, and he drove us in it back to the bridge and we watched as, expertly, he chained his truck to our car and hauled it safely to the other side of the bridge. We paid him the twenty-five dollars he asked for, an awful lot in those days for fifteen minutes of work, and we went on our way.

On the whole, however, our trips went off smoothly, and as the children grew older we ventured still farther west to see the great beauty of America: the awesome Rocky Mountains, the equally awesome Grand Canyon, Yellowstone National Park with its snowcapped mountains and herds of wild animals and lakes and rivers—things our children, and Ruby and I too, had never seen before except in pictures in magazines. We drove as far west as California and stayed in San Francisco for two days, enjoying its hilly streets, the mists that came often, and the streetcar ride that was part of the sightseeing. We drove from there to a redwood forest, gasping in amazement at the enormous size of these huge trees.

We felt a deep satisfaction at all of this, and we were glad to have been able to show our children part of the reason why America was such a great country. But there was one thing we did not show them, and that was the ugliness that existed in America also. There was a good opportunity to do this when Paul Robeson gave a concert in Peekskill, New York. Ruby and I were going with friends, and I am glad that we did not take Charlie and Adraenne with us because of what happened at that concert. I will tell you about this later.

Chapter Twelve

I DON'T REALLY KNOW HOW LONG IT TOOK ME TO WRITE *THE INVISIBLE Wall*. It must have been about a year, but it was finally done, and the next thing was to try to get it published. But did I really want to go into that sort of thing again? I hesitated before sending it out to a publisher. I'd done this hundreds of times before and always met with failure, a polite rejection note, or nothing at all. Was there any reason to think that things had changed?

For quite some time I kept the manuscript on my desk, satisfied with what I'd done, thinking I should leave well enough alone. The writing had done its job. I had been functioning normally. The grief was still there, but it was no longer as acute as it had been before. I could look at one of the photographs of Ruby on a wall or a table without crying. The loneliness and the terrible emptiness would always be there. I knew that would never pass. But why let myself in for the disappointments that I knew would inevitably come with submitting my manuscript to some editor who would have little interest in my life as a young boy in a Lancashire mill town?

I could never forget those disappointments. They were like wounds inflicted on my body, leaving scars. I think the worst of them all was the time Clifton Fadiman, the editor of Simon and Schuster, had shown some interest in my work after reading one of my short stories in a little magazine and had written me a letter inviting me to submit a novel.

Ruby and I had just been married, and writing and becoming a famous author were matters of life or death with me. I was thrilled by the letter, and I sat down immediately to write a novel that was doomed to failure because I didn't know how to write a novel. Nevertheless, I dashed one off in a few weeks, sent it off to Fadiman, and waited impatiently for the reply, rushing downstairs every time the mailman came to see if there was a letter for me from the publisher. Well, there was one day, and it was from Fadiman, and it asked me briefly to come in and see him about my novel.

I was in seventh heaven that day, absolutely certain that he would not have asked to see me unless it was to tell me that he was going to publish my novel. If it had been turned down, I reasoned, it would have come back to me with the usual polite rejection slip. It was on that positive note I went out and bought a bottle of wine to celebrate the occasion. When Ruby came home and heard the news she was as delighted as I was, and when we sat down to dinner—a meatloaf I had thrown together at the last moment from her written instructions—we toasted my success.

The following day I went to the office of Simon and Schuster filled with confidence. Fadiman, a bespectacled scholarly-looking man then in his early thirties, greeted me warmly, which heightened my assurance still more. But in a few moments all my expectations crumbled as I heard him tell me that he still had faith in me as a coming writer of talent, but the novel I'd submitted to him didn't fit his list. And where had I heard that before?

I could never forget that letdown. It was the worst of all the rejections I had received, and there were plenty more of them after that. Nor could I forget the many others like me who I met during this troubled period in my life. The first apartment Ruby and I rented after graduating from furnished rooms was in Greenwich Village, and it was there I met so many like myself who were struggling to become famous writers but had not yet had anything published. We often gathered on an evening to read one another's manuscripts and criticize them or perhaps to sit and commiserate with one another over our failures.

I can recall the greetings on these evenings when we met. They were generally the same each time.

"Ah, how are you? How's the writing going?"

"Oh, so-so."

"Any acceptance?" (A short laugh.) "Any interesting letters from editors?"

"No. How about you?"

"Same."

"Well, I guess we've got to keep plugging away."

"I guess so."

Many of these gatherings—soirees, they were called—took place in the apartment of a man by the name of James Deutsch. He was an escapee from Hitler's Germany, but insisted he was not Jewish and spoke often of his Aryan background. He had changed his name from whatever it was in Germany to Deutsch when he came to the United States, not realizing that Deutsch was a fairly common Jewish name in America. Still, he had done well here. He had become comptroller of a large department store. But he was a dignified and quite respectable comptroller only by day; by night he became a bohemian and a playwright, author of several unproduced plays.

Compared to the rest of us, who were either at low-paying jobs or jobless altogether in those Depression days, James was quite well off, and he was liberal with his expensive Scotch, which he himself consumed in great quantity without ever seeming drunk, smoking cigarettes incessantly at the same time. His place was also well stocked with forty-year-old cognac and liqueurs for the ladies, and so it was not surprising that his apartment—his studio, he preferred to call it—was always well filled.

It was filled the first time Ruby and I went there. We had been invited by James's wife, Hilda, who was a friend of Ruby's. It was on Waverly Place, in an ancient building that had an iron spiral stairway leading up to the top floor, where James and Hilda lived. We had arrived late, and we had to enter quietly, for James, wearing some sort of a blousy artist's smock and a large black bow tie, holding a glass of Scotch in one hand and a manuscript in the other, a cigarette burning in an ashtray on the floor beside him, was reading one of his plays in a voice that still had a strong German accent. All the lights in the room were off and candles burned here and there for illumination, so it was hard to see faces, and I could barely make out the circle of people surrounding James, seated or sprawled out on the floor.

There were some seats still left, and Hilda, seeing us, put a finger to her lips and led us tiptoeing to empty spots on a sofa. I tried to listen to the play, but soon realized how bad it was, and gave up listening and wished I hadn't come.

We stayed only because Ruby didn't want to offend Hilda, and with the Scotch and cognac flowing generously, the reading quickly degenerated into something else. Soon James, his flushed and sweating face the only telltale sign of his drinking, assumed another role: lover. It was, I was told later, the usual happening at these gatherings—a kissing binge that he alone indulged in.

Seizing hold of an attractive woman, he would grip her tightly, swing her off her feet, and press his lips to hers, holding the kiss passionately before letting her down and going on to the next woman. While this was going on, the husbands of these women smiled tolerantly and feigned indifference. But when I saw him heading for Ruby I decided I wasn't going to be tolerant, and I got ready for him. As soon as he approached and reached out his hands for her, I sprang up from the sofa and put myself in between them, facing him.

"You touch her," I said, "and I'll kill you."

He stared at me openmouthed, as if he couldn't believe what he was hearing. The whole room had grown silent. Nobody spoke like that to James, not with all that Scotch around. But James backed off. He gave a little bow, and for a moment I thought he was going to click his heels, but instead he turned on them and walked over to the table, where he poured himself another Scotch and lit another cigarette.

Ruby and I left shortly afterward, and as soon as we got outside, Ruby bent forward and burst into hysterical laughter. I joined her, and we both had a good laugh out of the episode.

But the results of some other literary endeavors weren't so funny. One in particular ended tragically. I'd tried not to think of this one because it was so painful, but it had clung to me all through the years, and now especially it came back in full force. His name was Jerry something or other. I have forgotten the last name, but that doesn't matter. He was about my age then, in his early twenties, and we had gone to high school together in Chicago, where I lived for a number of years before coming to New York. Jerry and I had scarcely known each other then. We weren't in any of the same classes, and only saw each other occasionally and nodded without ever speaking to each other. He always struck me as being morose and pretty much of a loner, and this had not changed when I met him by accident in New York as I was leaving the Fifth Avenue library and he was going in.

We recognized each other immediately, and stopped to shake hands and talk briefly since he did not show any desire to prolong the meeting. But it was long enough for me to learn that he too was a writer, or rather that he was trying to become one and was working on a novel, and that he lived in the Bronx with his widowed mother not far from where I lived with my parents. This was another coincidence, and I took advantage of it because I was curious about him and wished I had gotten to know him better at school, aware now that he was a writer. I went to see him and I think he was glad to see me, though he did not show any great enthusiasm. But he did not have any friends and did not go anyplace other than libraries, and he must have been lonely, so he appreciated my visit.

I met his mother too. She gave me a much warmer greeting and was obviously glad to see that he had made a friend. She was a tiny woman—*petite* is perhaps a better word to describe her—with snow-white hair and yet a clear, unwrinkled complexion. Her two sharp, bright eyes often gazed up worshipfully at her son, who was a giant in comparison. Clearly, she doted on him—her husband had died several years ago of a heart attack and Jerry was all she had, and she believed that he was a genius.

She let me know that soon enough that first time I went to see them in their top-floor apartment in one of the big apartment houses that are packed into the Bronx. She served coffee and cake, and as she did so she said in a voice that rarely rose above a whisper, "He is not just a writer but a great writer, and when his book is published he will be known as the genius that he is. I read a great deal myself. I used to be an English teacher, and reading books was part of my work, but I have never come upon an author who could compare to Jerry. He has been working on his book now for over six years. He started it when he was still in high school, and I knew from the first moment that it was going to be a great book. And it is. He is almost finished with it, and I am looking over the publishers to find who is the best one for him. He should have only the best. He rates it, and the whole world will agree. I am sure of it."

Jerry was sitting opposite me at the table, and he was taking this in with his eyes cast down gloomily to the floor. I don't know how he was feeling about all this praise, but it certainly aroused my curiosity, and I asked if I could read some of his book.

I think the mother was about to say "Certainly," but Jerry interrupted, bellowing, "No!"

Later on, when we were alone for a few moments, Jerry having gone to the bathroom, she apologized to me, saying Jerry never let anyone read his manuscript, not even her, and she had only been taking its greatness for granted because she had been convinced of his genius from the time he was a child and whatever he did or wrote had to be exceptional.

I only saw him a few times after that. Except for the writing we had little in common, and he was always so morose and gloomy he was not particularly pleasant to be with. I had friends in the Village and I introduced him to some of them, but these meetings did not go off so well because of his disagreeable manner and his antisocial behavior, so I soon put an end to that and began to see less and less of him.

Then one day, having nothing to do, I decided to go and visit him. If I had read the newspapers a few days before I would have been better prepared for what I was going to learn after I'd climbed those endless steps and reached the top floor, breathless. I knocked on the door and Jerry's mother opened it, and the moment I saw her I knew something was wrong. She was wearing a kimono and her white hair was in disarray, as if she had just gotten out of bed, and she had been crying.

"Is Jerry in?" I asked.

She stood looking at me for a moment, clutching the edges of the kimono together, and her eyes were watery. Then she said brokenly, "Come in, please." And after I had done so and she had closed the door behind me, she said in the same voice, "Jerry's dead."

It was a shock. I stared at her, and said, "I'm sorry. When did it happen?"

"A week ago," she said, and seemed to have difficulty talking. She wiped her eyes with a tissue she was holding in her hand. "I came into his room and he was hanging."

This stunned me. At first I didn't quite understand. "What do you mean," I asked, "you found him hanging?"

"He hanged himself," she said, and began crying.

I went up to her and put an arm around her, and said, "I can't believe this. Tell me what happened."

I got her to sit down, and she wept more, telling me how it had happened, and why. It was because of his novel. He had finally finished it, and she chose a publisher for him and mailed it off for him.

"And I was so happy," she said. "I think he was too, though, you know, he never showed happiness. But he'd spent all these years writing it, and it was finally over, and now he was going to get the rewards that he deserved. It would be a big success. I was sure of it. It would be acclaimed by all the critics. He would be recognized as one of America's greatest writers. I told him that, and I think he believed me and felt that way himself. You know, you couldn't tell much by looking at his face, and he never talked much about what he was thinking, but a mother's instinct told me everything about him. I knew that he couldn't wait to hear from the publisher. He knew when the mailman came and he'd always find some excuse to be downstairs at that time. And then one day he came back upstairs with a package in his hand. He was walking very slowly. I asked him what it was. He didn't answer. He just threw his package onto the table and went into his bedroom and closed the door. He knew what it was. I did too when I looked at the return address on the label. It was from the publisher I had sent it to. I opened it. I had to. Yes, it was the manuscript, and there was a slip of paper with it that said it had been rejected as unsuitable for their list."

She had to stop then because she was weeping so hard, and her voice broke down completely. I comforted her as best I could, and she was able to go on after a while. "I couldn't believe it at first. It just didn't seem possible. There had to be some mistake. I wanted to call up the publisher and ask whoever was in authority there. But I thought I ought to get Jerry's permission first. I knocked on his door and he didn't answer. I opened the door and peeped in, and then I saw him. . . ."

She simply could not go on, and I did not urge her to do so. There was no need to. I knew now what she had seen, and I knew why it had happened. The newspaper account, which I read later in the library, did not give that explanation for his suicide, but merely said that he had been despondent and had been suffering from depression for some time.

Before I left, Jerry's mother insisted that I take the manuscript of his novel and see for myself whether it was not the work of genius that she still insisted it was. I was curious enough to want to read it, and I took it home with me in the wrapper of the publisher that had sent it back to him. And I did read it, or as much of it as I was able to.

If I had been a reader then, as I was later, for motion picture companies, reading all sorts of manuscripts—book, plays, stories, a wide variety of stuff—for consideration as movies, I might have been less puzzled than I was with Jerry's book. Much of what I later had to read was what you might call literary junk, but I don't think anything I ever read was as puzzling as this one.

Perhaps I can best describe it by comparing it to an abstract painting where the colors are vivid and dramatic but the meaning, if any, is clear only to the painter. The sentences in Jerry's book were clear enough and well written, but there was no connection between the sentences, and collectively they made no sense. It seemed like a lot of gibberish to me. There were over five hundred pages of this confusion to the manuscript, and I could struggle through only ten of them before I gave up.

And it was for this, I thought, that Jerry had hanged himself. But how many more were there like him? Not all of them had hanged themselves in frustration and deadened hopes, but their lives had been soured by the efforts and disappointments. I could think of any number of them besides Jerry. There was Thelma, comfortably married to a doctor, the mother of a young boy, who gave it all up to come to Greenwich Village to write; she failed, but she could never go back to her husband and son. There was Fred, a pharmacist who

110

HARRY BERNSTEIN

gave up his job to come to the Village to work as a janitor in an apartment house where he could get free rent and write. There were people who made all sorts of sacrifices to become writers but did not succeed and could never adjust to the conventional life of just an ordinary person.

I was one of them myself. But my suffering was less than any of theirs because of Ruby. She made my life so pleasant and so easy to bear that nothing else counted. Now Ruby was no longer with me, however, and I buried myself in my writing once again. Only this time it was not the all-consuming thing it had once been; it had served as therapy and to some extent gotten my mind off my grief. Once *The Invisible Wall* was finished, I remembered my past efforts and those of people I had once known, including the tragic figure of my ex-schoolmate who had hanged himself, and I questioned whether it was worth once again going through all that struggle to find a publisher, a process with inevitable rejections and bitter disappointments. *Let well enough alone,* I told myself. *Be satisfied with what you have accomplished. You are emotionally better off than before. You can think of Ruby without choking up. Get busy on another book. There is plenty more to write about.* I told myself all that, and let my finished manuscript lie on my desk untouched for several weeks.

Then one day I went out for a walk around the lake, the walk Ruby and I had taken every day, hand in hand—only now I discovered something new about myself and what it was like to be in my nineties.

Chapter Thirteen

2004

FOR THE GREATER PART OF THE YEAR WHILE I WAS WORKING ON MY book I had been sedentary, sitting at my desk most of the time pounding away at my typewriter, so I had no inkling that anything was wrong until I went out to take my walk around the lake. It was spring, beautiful weather. The trees were budding and early flowers were beginning to show, the crocuses and the hyacinths peeping up out of the earth and the yellow forsythia already blooming in clumps here and there.

I felt a burst of energy as I stepped out of the house, and looked forward to a good long walk. I only wished Ruby were with me. But there was no use wishing that. It could never happen. I felt a certain stiffness in my legs as I crossed the street and went down to the lake, but I thought that was simply due to lack of exercise and after a while the stiffness would ease up. It didn't, however, and as a matter of fact only grew worse, and very soon I had to sit down on a bench. I rested a few minutes, then got up to try again, and this time as I did so I lost my balance and fell. Luckily, it was grass I fell onto, so there was no serious injury, but I had a great deal of trouble getting up onto my feet.

There would be quite a number of falls after this, and I would learn eventually that the best way to get back up was to turn onto my stomach, then get on my hands and knees and straighten up bit by bit. This is one of the many tricks the nonagenarian has to learn in order to cope with the inevitable muscular weakening that takes place in all of us.

I learned that from my doctor. I had gone to him after my first fall, and he explained it to me, and also advised me to start using a cane when I walked.

"In fact," he said, "you might also start thinking of getting a walker."

I laughed, and very emphatically I said, "Oh, no!" I'd seen old people—I always called them that—creeping around bent over and holding on to one of those things on wheels that looked like baby carriages. "That's not for me," I said. Even then, well into my nineties, I still could not picture myself being that old and decrepit.

He looked at me thoughtfully for a moment, then asked, "How long do you think you have to live?"

I thought it was a peculiar question, and did not know how to answer it for a moment. Finally I said, "Shouldn't you know the answer to that better than I?"

"Sometimes," he said, "when patients get to your age, which is ninety-four, they know the answer better than I do. I can guess in some cases, but in your case, I wouldn't want to do that. You're in reasonably good health, you have no observable life-threatening diseases; you could go on for quite few years. But I do know that this weakening of the muscles that you have will not go away, but will in fact increase in different parts of your body. So don't turn your nose up at a walker. If you want to live, it will help you do so. Just thank your lucky stars it doesn't have to be a wheelchair. A lot of people your age have to settle for that."

He was absolutely right. The fall I had suffered that day was only the first of several that followed in the succeeding months, and two or three of those times I had to be taken to an emergency room to have torn skin stitched and X-rays taken. I was luckier than most elderly, to whom a fall meant a fractured bone, particularly the hip. I got away with minor injuries, but I also came to the realization that I needed help of some sort in walking. I could no longer walk around the lake, and that was a serious blow to me. It had meant so much to me, the one thing Ruby and I had always done together but which I could do alone, always accompanied by memories of her and her hand in mine as we walked.

And yet I still resisted the doctor's advice to get a walker. I was not ready for it yet, even though I began to find it difficult merely to stand on my feet, and had to grasp hold of something to steady myself.

It was my son and his wife, Marcy, who took matters into their own hands and presented me with a walker as a surprise gift, assuming that I would welcome it.

I didn't. I was furious. "Who needs that?" I said. "Take it back to the store."

They didn't argue. But they left it there with me to think about, and I glanced at it now and then with dislike but growing interest. I had seen walkers before, with old men and women crouched over them, but they were nothing like this one. This was the latest thing in walkers. It had a seat on which you could rest when you got tired. The seat lifted up and inside there was a pocket for storing things such as refreshments or groceries if you went shopping. It also had a brake. I began to test it out, and eventually I found myself using it without feeling self-conscious in public, pleased with the mobility it gave me.

Today, it is an indispensable part of the equipment for my nineties, which includes a variety of canes, a pair of crutches just in case, a bathtub seat, an alert button that will bring aid in case I fall and can't get up, and a first-aid kit.

But I was less prepared for emergencies at the time I finished writing my book, even though I was already ninety-four. I was in good shape physically. People refused to believe my age when I told it to them. But I had spent months indoors working on the book, and it was not until I got outside and began to move around that I noticed the change that had taken place in my physical condition. Perhaps that contributed to the feeling of gloom and discouragement that came over me after I had finished my book. Quite clearly I had only a limited amount of time left. That was what the doctor had been hinting at. So what difference did it make if I sent the book out and it got kicked back to me? What difference did anything make?

So it was with this attitude that I started sending *The Invisible Wall* out to publishers, trying to tell myself that no matter what happened, I didn't give a damn.

Chapter Fourteen

1949

THE POLITICAL CLIMATE HAD CHANGED CONSIDERABLY IN THE United States since the war ended, and the Soviet Union, once our ally in the war against Hitler, was now considered the enemy in what was called the Cold War. Right-wing thinking was prevalent throughout the country, and because the famous African American singer Paul Robeson was an outspoken advocate of the Soviet Union, he was regarded generally as a Communist and one of the enemy. Reactionary groups such as the Ku Klux Klan joined forces with veterans' organizations in Peekskill, New York, to prevent a planned concert for Robeson from taking place, and when the first attempt was made on August 29, 1949, to hold the concert they disrupted it with a violent attack on the audience, and a riot followed that lasted several hours with many cars smashed and people injured.

The supporters of Robeson, who included Communists, Socialists, liberals, and union members, refused to give up, and a second attempt was planned for a week later, the first Sunday of September. It was to this concert that Ruby and I were invited to attend with our friends, Fred and Myra, a couple we had known since our days in the Village, both of them writers and both liberals. They assured us that this was not a Communist affair, knowing how opposed Ruby and I were to the Communists, but was being backed by all Americans who believed in freedom of speech, and this meant many thousands. Further, they assured us, there would be adequate police protection this time to prevent what had taken place last time.

It seemed safe enough to us, and we could hardly miss an opportunity to hear Paul Robeson sing. There would also be Pete Seeger on the program, a favorite folk singer of ours. Just the same, we stuck to our decision to not take the kids along, and they would be well taken care of by Aunt Lily.

Sunday, September 3, 1949, began as a beautiful bright, sunny day. Ruby and I were up early. It had been decided after much argument that we would drive up to Peekskill in Fred's car. I had wanted to use mine, but Fred was insistent, so I let him have his way, and that meant Ruby and I would have to take a bus and then a subway into New York. It made little sense, but I would find out later why Fred was so insistent on taking his car. I would also find out the true reason why he asked me to bring a baseball bat along. He'd told me the concert was being held out in the open on some picnic grounds on the outskirts of Peekskill, and it would be part picnic, with a lunch Myra was packing, and there might be a chance of getting a baseball game going.

It was not that at all, but then I never even suspected anything else, and I had to ask Charlie if I could take his baseball bat along. He seemed surprised.

"I thought you were going to a concert," he said.

"We are," I assured him, and then explained what Fred had told me.

"Then why can't I go?" Charlie asked.

It looked as if we were going to have a bit of trouble. There was nothing Charlie liked better than to go someplace. But fortunately, Aunt Lily arrived just then and told them she and Peo were going to take them to Jones Beach, and that settled it. Charlie loved to swim and there was no more fuss. Later on I realized how close I had been to giving in and how disastrous that would have been.

But there was little thought of disaster when the four of us started out from Greenwich Village, where Fred and Myra still lived. We were all in high spirits. Fred's car was an older-model Plymouth that had lost most of its green color, and it was not as comfortable as mine would have been. Fred and Myra sat in the front, Ruby and I in the back on seats that were dented and hard. With the baseball bat and the packages of food both Myra and Ruby had brought, there wasn't too much leg room for me, but I didn't mind. It was such a beautiful day, and we were looking forward to hearing Pete Seeger and Paul Robeson—especially Robeson. We talked about him as we drove. Myra had met him one time when she was interviewing him for a magazine she once worked for. Turning around in her seat, she told us of the wonderful experience it had been for her meeting this giant of a man whose singing had always captivated her, and hearing from him the story of his life.

It was not at the start very different from the life of any black man in America at this time, a time when segregation was legal in America and black people were being lynched by white mobs, especially in the South. Paul Robeson was born in Princeton, New Jersey, the youngest of five children. His father was a runaway slave who went on to graduate from Lincoln University, his mother a Quaker who fought for the abolition of slavery, and so it was a family that suffered hardship but with a determination to rise above it.

"And Paul certainly did," Myra told me. "In 1915 he won a four-year scholarship to Rutgers University, and there he also excelled in sports, and despite all the violence and racism that came from teammates, he won fifteen varsity letters in sports, baseball, basketball, track, and he was twice named to the all-American football team. And he was Phi Beta Kappa."

She shook her head, still in wonder with all this, and Ruby and I, hearing it for the first time, felt the same way as she did. But how had he come to be a singer? we wanted to know.

Music, she explained, was still far from his mind when he came out of Rutgers. He planned to become a lawyer, and entered Columbia Law School, where he met and married Eslanda Cordoza Goode, who was the first black woman to head a pathology laboratory. After graduation he took a job with a law firm but left when a white secretary refused to take dictation from him. It was then he decided to leave law altogether and use his artistic talents and his fine deep baritone voice to promote African American history and culture. This eventually led to his triumph in such operas as *Emperor Jones* and *Othello,* and especially with the black spirituals that had been virtually forgotten until he resurrected them on the stage.

There was one other thing that meant more than anything else to him: the struggle for freedom by the black people. This is what he said to Myra that day, "The artist must take sides. He must elect to fight for freedom or slavery. I have made my choice. I had no alternative."

"When you think of all the success he had as a singer, and how comfortable his life could have been and the wealth he could have had," said Myra, "you've got to admire him for sticking his neck out in the struggle for freedom the way he did, and for daring to say that there was more freedom in the Soviet Union than there was in the United States. You know about that, don't you?"

"Who doesn't?" murmured Fred at the wheel.

Yes, who didn't know that Robeson had said it? It was for that reason many people had come to believe that he was a Communist, and in turn many of his concerts had been canceled and much of his once worshipful audiences had turned against him. It was because of this also that residents of Peekskill were opposed to his giving a concert there, and rednecks and Ku Kluxers, taking advantage of the situation and with the local press encouraging them, had formed the mob that prevented the previous week's concert from taking place.

It had been in all the newspapers all over the country, with editorials supporting the rising tide against the black singer. Ruby and I had read about it and couldn't help but be influenced by it, though not completely. It did look to us as if Robeson, if not a Communist, was a sympathizer, and we had no love for Communists and couldn't agree with Robeson's assessment that the Soviet Union had greater freedom than the United States.

How could anyone say that? We had discussed it between ourselves. Russia was under the rule of Stalin, as cruel a dictator as Hitler or Mussolini, and it could not be compared to the United States, despite the fact that we knew the blacks had never been treated fairly here. People here were at least allowed to say what they wanted about things, just as Myra was doing now, but in the Soviet Union they could be sent to prison for speaking openly about anything they disagreed with.

Yet listening to Myra now, Ruby and I began to feel uncomfortable. We wanted to contradict her, but we knew that would spark a political argument, and we did not want to spoil our day. It was bright and beautiful and there was much to look forward to, so we remained silent, and soon anyway the topic changed to something else, and perhaps also Fred and Myra knew how we felt. We'd had discussions before on similar subjects concerning the Communists and there'd been some very serious arguments. They were not, as they assured us, Communists themselves, but they felt there were ample reasons to side with them at times.

We liked them both just the same, and our liking had grown with the years, and they had been out to Laurelton to visit us several times. Nothing could spoil that friendship. We all felt so on that day.

IN THE MEANTIME, we had driven a good part of the way. We had left the city behind and were driving north on the parkway through the rolling hills of Westchester, and now and then we caught glimpses of the Hudson River glittering through the trees. Both Fred and Myra were familiar with the area, having visited friends often in the summer colonies that surrounded the Peekskill area. In addition, they had been here only a week ago, so Fred knew the roads well and pretty soon he turned off the parkway and onto a back road that would enable us to reach the picnic grounds without having to go through Peekskill.

It was a narrow, bumpy dirt road that wound among the hills, with heavy woods on either side, and occasionally here and there a clearing with a shack showing and a clothesline strung across a yard and some ragged kids staring at us. I thought of Tobacco Road but didn't say anything.

After a few miles of this road Fred turned onto a wider main road and said we had only another mile or so to go. I felt some apprehension as we approached the entrance to the picnic grounds. We were not the only ones arriving, even though it was early. There were many cars ahead of us and several buses loaded with people, most of them African Americans and all singing and in a gay mood. Still, a distance from the entrance we slowed down and the line crawled bumper to bumper, and then we saw the mob gathered around the entrance and heard their ugly shouts and threats. For a while it seemed as if my apprehension was justified, and I could feel Ruby's alarm as she moved closer to me and put her hand in mine.

However, we were reassured by the sight of the police at the gate, who were seeing to it that the cars and buses got through. Later we learned that some of the arriving people fell into the hands of the mob. These were largely African Americans, and some of them were pulled out of their cars and beaten.

However, not knowing that at the time, we felt once we were inside the grounds that there was nothing to worry about, and indeed it was a reassuring sight to see so many people there already, thousands of them, with buses and cars already taking up many of the parking spaces. Furthermore, guards, most of them volunteer union men, were posted all around the perimeter of the grounds, and additional guards were lined around the sound truck from which Paul Robeson and Pete Seeger would sing. Then, too, we were further reassured when we saw a small army of state troopers arriving.

Nothing could happen to us, we thought, and having found a comfortable spot on the side of a hill, we began to enjoy our Sunday picnic. Others were doing the same thing around us, and Fred and Myra knew some of them and waved to them, and several came over and we were introduced to them, and all felt as we did that things looked promising for the concert to be heard this time without the interruption that had taken place at the previous week's attempt.

And then, as we were talking, we noticed that the sound truck was being moved from its position where it was most visible to the huge audience to a spot nearby under a huge oak tree whose branches would obscure the view for most people.

We were all puzzled. Why would they want to do that? One of the men went to find out, and came back with the answer. Several scouts from security had found two snipers hiding behind bushes on a hill overlooking the sound truck where it had been before. They were armed with telescopic rifles and obviously planned to kill Paul Robeson. They'd been driven off, but there could be a further attempt, and to protect Robeson as much as possible they had decided to move the truck to where the singer would be less of an easy target.

It brought back a lot of the uneasiness Ruby and I had felt before, but Fred and Myra made light of the matter, pointing out that with the arrival of the state troopers nobody would take a chance on killing Robeson out in the open and in broad daylight. And there was so much fun and laughter going on around us. Children were scampering around playing games, reminding me of the baseball bat I had brought and left in the car. I reminded Fred of it, and he said there wasn't enough time left for a ball game. It looked as if the concert was about to begin.

A tall man wearing a jacket and tie came out onto the sound truck to announce the singers and the program, and the picnic grounds grew quiet and the children went back to their parents. Fred whispered to me that the man was Howard Fast, a well-known writer whose books I had read and admired. I found out later that he was chairman of the concert and had been in the forefront of the battle with the mob the previous week. Nevertheless, even though he knew he was risking his own life, he had organized this concert, determined to show the mob, whom he called fascists, that he and the audience were not afraid of them.

He spoke briefly and in a quiet, firm voice, giving a short background of the performers, and then the concert began. Whatever uneasiness might have remained in our minds vanished as we listened enthralled first to Pete Seeger's folk songs and then to the spirituals in Robeson's voice, which had the deep, rolling quality of an organ.

Suddenly there came an interruption, the loud, throbbing noise of an engine, and everybody looked up to see a helicopter flying low over the sound truck. There were police markings on it. Fury swept over everyone as the helicopter, apparently quite deliberately, went back and forth. But a smile came over Robeson's face and he went on singing, and someone adjusted the volume on the microphone system to make his voice more audible to everyone. Apparently realizing that their attempt to drown him out had failed, the helicopter eventually left.

So once more we were caught up in the magic of the great singer's voice, and when it was over there was thunderous applause. We all rose, satisfied that we had accomplished what we came for and that the mob had been defeated this time.

By this time I had begun to feel as Fred and Myra did, as so many of the audience did, that this was more than just a concert. It was a challenge to the rednecks and Ku Klux Klan, who made up the largest part of the mob, an assertion that we had the right to free speech and we were willing to fight for it. I think Ruby felt the same way, although in the light of what was to follow, we would wonder if this same thing could not have been accomplished in a simpler, more peaceful fashion.

But we were not thinking of that as we left. We were jubilant over what we considered a triumph, and we joined the crowds heading for the parking lot, and got into the car, looking forward to a pleasant ride home, to coming up to Fred and Myra's apartment for coffee, and then home to our kids.

"Glad you came?" Fred asked as he got behind the wheel.

"Yes," I said, "damned glad," forgetting all about the earlier fears when we first came and saw the mob at the entrance, then the shift of the sound truck to the oak tree, and the helicopter.

It was still early, only about five o'clock, the sun lower in the sky but still blazing. The car had no air-conditioning, and so the windows were wide open. As we got into the line of cars heading for the entrance, now the exit, a security guard went from car to car saying, "Keep your windows closed as you leave."

He did not explain why, but Fred obeyed and told us to close our windows in the back. I think he knew why but did not want to alarm us. It took quite a long time to reach the gates, and we crawled forward behind the cars ahead of us at a snail's pace. Finally as we reached the gates we understood why the windows had to be closed.

The mob that had greeted us as we came in had increased by hundreds, and the state police who were stationed there did little to prevent them from surging forward toward the departing cars and blocking their way out, shouting curses, epithets, and profanities, fists banging on the doors and windows. But that was only the start. Fred managed to crawl past them only to find that the road to the right on which he had intended to turn had been blocked with piles of stone, making it necessary for him to turn left onto a narrow road. All the cars had been forced to do the same thing, and once on that road the horrors really began.

From the distance there came to us the sounds of splintering glass, screams, shouts, and the crying of children. Soon a rock came crashing through our side window, showering us with fragments of glass. We all let out cries and tried to brush ourselves off.

I remember yelling to Fred, "Can't you turn off somewhere?"

"No, I can't," came Fred's desperate answer.

We were all trapped on this road and compelled to run a gauntlet that had been cunningly set up for us. Stationed at intervals on either side of the road were groups of men, women, even youngsters gleefully joining the attack, all armed with piles of stones and bricks that they hurled at the slowly passing cars and buses. Their taunts sounded in my ears clearly above all the other clamor, the smashing of glass, the thumping and beating of fists and clubs against the metal of the cars.

"Nigger bastards."

"Jew sons of bitches. Go back to New York."

"Hitler didn't do enough."

Yes, I heard that too, and it gave a clue as to the makeup of the mob. I heard this: "We're going to finish where Hitler left off."

The destruction was terrible. Some cars were turned over and their occupants beaten as they lay on the ground. Children were screaming and crying, but there was no mercy for anyone—the children were beaten too. I remember looking around desperately for the police. They were there, all right, I saw them, but they were doing nothing to stop the onslaught. In fact, I saw them take part in it. When Fred was forced momentarily to a halt, a fat trooper beat on our window with his club and yelled, "Get going, you Jew bastard."

And when we couldn't, he smashed another one of the windows with his club and then laughed.

If I ever felt like killing someone, it was at that moment. And yet until then there could not have been a stronger champion of the police than I was. I'd believed we relied on them for the safety of our lives, that they were our only means of protection against the criminal element, and that they were brave men who put their own lives on the line to save other people. But all that changed after I witnessed what was going on there, with state troopers actually taking part in the riot against people who had done nothing more than attend a concert. I saw them throwing rocks at the cars and buses and laughing as they did so.

But as sick and furious as I felt then, the important thing was to get out of the trap we were in—and also, as we discovered, to get some medical attention for Fred. He had been badly cut in the hand from flying glass and was bleeding all over the steering wheel. Myra had received cuts too, but she did not know how to drive a car even if it had been possible for her to take over for Fred. Fortunately, Ruby and I had escaped any injury and either one of us could drive. But if we stopped to change over, they would pounce on us like hunting dogs on their prey.

Fortunately, we did not have much farther to go before the nightmare was over and we were able to drive without any more injury. But now as we got back onto the main road, I was able to take over at the wheel, and we began to look for a hospital because we had nothing that could stop the bleeding of Fred's hand, and Myra's cuts needed tending to also.

There was a policeman directing traffic at one corner and I stopped and asked him if he could direct us to a hospital. He looked at me before answering, he looked at the car and saw the damages on it and guessed where we had come from. Word of the riot had spread all over by now and was headline news in newspapers all over the country, in fact, all over the world.

A look of contempt had come on the officer's face, and he said, "We got no hospitals 'round here." He meant "for you."

"But there's got to be one," I argued. "There's a man seriously injured."

"If you don't get going," he said, "I'll give you a ticket."

We drove on, and only two blocks away I saw the hospital and drove into Emergency. We were not the only ones coming from the concert. The place was filled with others who had been caught by the mob, and the one nurse on duty was cold and unpleasant.

"Why don't you people stay home where you belong?" she said.

This, in addition to the long wait we'd have to suffer made Fred decide he didn't want their medical attention. We did get the nurse to give us some bandages and we at least managed to stop some of the bleeding, which obviously needed stitching. Ruby did the bandaging well enough for the time being, and we left.

I drove back to New York, and since it was so late already, and since we were anxious to get home and clean ourselves up and discard clothes that still contained bits of glass and whatever else had been thrown at us, we left Fred and Myra at their apartment, Fred apologizing profusely for having gotten us into this thing, and I assuring him that we didn't blame him for anything and that perhaps we had learned a great deal from our experience, and that no matter what had happened we had heard Paul Robeson sing, and that really was all that mattered.

I think I meant it. But what really mattered now was to get home, and never had I felt such urgent desire for my home as I did then. It took us another hour and a half to get back to Laurelton, and

Ruby felt as I did—that we couldn't wait to get into that ugly brick bungalow of ours, where we felt safe and comfortable and happy.

The children were in their beds asleep, and Aunt Lily and Peo were sitting waiting for us anxiously. They knew all about the Peekskill riot—the whole world knew about it by now, as the news had been broadcast over the radio and was in all the late-night newspapers. Lily and Peo had been afraid we might have been caught in it. Well, we had, and we told them about our experience. Lily listened with horror on her face, but Peo's face was an expressionless mask. I knew, however, what he was thinking. He had been through a lot of similar battles in his years with the IWW. If he were to voice his feelings now, it would be in a bitter tone, and he would say, "What else is new in the capitalist world?"

But he said nothing. What a good thing it was we hadn't taken the children to the concert, Lily remarked, and she told us of the wonderful time they'd had at Jones Beach, and how quickly and willingly they had gone to bed, so pleasantly tired they were from their swimming.

As soon as Lily and Peo had gone, and before Ruby and I did anything else, we went to look at our children.

First, Adraenne in the downstairs bedroom next to ours. We opened the door quietly and tiptoed into the room. She was fast asleep with a thumb in her mouth. Each of us in turn bent down and kissed her lightly, then tiptoed out of the room.

Charlie next. We went softly up the stairs and opened the door. You could never tell what to expect with him. No matter how late it was, he could be up and reading a forbidden comic magazine. But no, he was sprawled out in his bed sound asleep, the blanket thrown aside, apparently well relaxed, as Adraenne was, from their swim.

Ruby adjusted the blanket over him, and we both kissed him lightly, then left the room.

We tiptoed down the stairs, and when we got to the bottom I put my arms around Ruby and whispered, "Aren't we lucky?"

"I was just thinking the same thing," she whispered back.

And then I kissed her, and we both stood there for a few moments, arms around each other, the same thought in our minds: how lucky we were, and how warm and safe the house was, and how glad we were to be in it.

Chapter Fifteen

2005

HISTORY REPEATED ITSELF AS I BEGAN SENDING MY BOOK TO PUB-lishers: Each time it was returned with the familiar polite note of re-jection. In the post office, however, I was something of a celebrity. The clerk who waited on me the first time I came there to send the book out, a tall, curly-haired fellow with a cheerful manner, asked what the package contained in order to determine the cost of ship-ping, and when I told him it was a book I had written, his eyes widened.

"Are you a writer?" he asked.

I nodded. I was a writer, wasn't I?

"Wow!" he said. "I've never met a writer before. I always wanted to be a writer."

I had met others like him before, people who wanted to be writers but somehow never got around to writing. The postal business was forgotten as we chatted away, with a line of customers waiting impatiently behind me. He told me about himself. He'd been a post office clerk for fifteen years. He was married. He had four children. He'd always sworn he'd quit his job and just write. But he'd stuck it out, and here he was, liking his work really, liking the customers and being liked by them, and not suffering too much from unrequited ambition.

I spoke more sparingly about myself, but I did tell him that I had once worked in the post office in Chicago and had written a story about my post office experiences, and the story had been published in a magazine called *The Anvil* about a million years ago. And once he knew that, he was stunned with admiration and wanted to read the story.

"Wow!" he kept saying. "Imagine that! Imagine writing a story about the post office! Imagine being published in a magazine. Wow!" He was so excited about it he insisted on telling his fellow clerks about it, and they were all impressed.

He begged me to bring the magazine in the next time I came, and I did. *The Anvil,* one of the more prominent little magazines of the 1930s, had long since ceased publication, and the copy I had, which also featured a story by Nelson Algren, was in a crumbly state, its pages turned yellow, but I gave it to him anyway, and I must say he took good care of it, and so did the others to whom he passed it on, and eventually it was returned to me in no worse condition than what it had been before.

But after seeing my name in print, the clerk was doubly excited about my being an author, and so were all the others, and from that time on I was treated as a celebrity. Whenever I came in with a book to mail there were respectful greetings, and my curly-haired friend hurried to be the one to wait on me and to talk about my latest achievement as a writer.

You see, I never let on that the book I was mailing out this time was the same one that I had mailed the month before. They assumed it was another book, and that I was a prolific writer who turned one out every month or so. It was another department at the post office that handled the book when it was returned from the publisher, so they had no way of knowing, and I saw no reason why I should disillusion them, and perhaps kill my friend's ambition to become a writer. I let him go on saying "Wow!"

Had I been in a better state of mind I could at least have gotten a smile out of it, but I was in no condition to be amused by anything. Despite all my determination not to let possible rejections hurt me, as they had done in my earlier writing efforts, I found they still hurt, and perhaps even more keenly than before because now I had to contend with something that I had not had to deal with before. It was old age.

Old age can be depressing in itself, with all its physical and emotional impairments, and with the knowledge constantly hanging over you that you are approaching the end of your life. My walking had reached the stage where I could not take a step without holding on to something. I was having trouble doing the things that were necessary to keep me alive: cook a decent meal, keep the house clean, shop for groceries, do the laundering. These things had always been done for me, but now I had to do them for myself, and often couldn't. I needed help, but I could not afford a housekeeper. Ruby and I had had a modest but comfortable income. When she died I lost a part of that. I was left with enough for myself but not enough to be able to afford someone to come in and help with all the things that had to be done.

I had been struggling with all of this ever since I began to live alone. Adraenne came every other week to stay with me for two days, and before she left she cooked enough meals to last for several days. Charles and his wife did much for me, insisting that I stay with them in their home in Pennsylvania for an occasional weekend. But it was not enough, and there were so many things for me to do it's a wonder I had time to write my book. And yet I did, though I did my writing during the night when I was unable to sleep.

And then soon there was another reason for my not being able to sleep: I woke up one night soaking wet. I was horrified when I realized what it was. I could not remember anything like that happening to me before, even when I was a child. Perhaps it had happened then often enough, as it did to all young children, but I could not possibly remember any of it, and I had escaped the miseries of some children as they grew up with bed-wetting.

I recall being so bewildered by what had happened that I simply did not know what to do. I recall getting out of bed and standing cold and shivering and wet, and my gaze fell on a photograph of Ruby that hung on a wall, a photograph of her I had taken from the balcony of a hotel when we were in New Orleans. It had been drizzling that morning, and she held a red umbrella over her head. I remember looking at her and saying miserably, "Ruby, what shall I do?"

So I was in a state a lot of people my age are in, and the continuous rejection of my book did not help. It occurred to me at this time that since my story was set in England, an English publisher might be more inclined to look at it favorably. When my curly-haired friend told me what the cost of mailing it to England was, I hesitated. It was an awful lot, and nine chances out of ten it would be sent back and the money would be wasted. Finally, I decided to gamble.

Then one day several weeks later I received a telephone call, and my whole life changed.

Chapter Sixteen

<u>1960</u>

THESE WERE TURBULENT TIMES IN AMERICAN HISTORY. IT WAS JUST after the McCarthy era and the mad hunt for suspected Communists, the blacklisting of famous Hollywood actors and writers, with the Cold War heating up to the 1961 Bay of Pigs fiasco, and then, in 1962, the Cuban missile crisis. The young president John F. Kennedy had said with a smiling face, declaring, "Ask not what your country can do for you, but what you can do for your country." Then the smiling face was blotted out of existence as he and his beautiful wife were driving in an open touring car in a parade through the streets of Dallas, Texas, and rifle shots rang out, and the face slumped to one side and the beautiful wife screamed and tried to scramble out of the car.

Events came one after another in rapid and deadly succession. It was like a roaring sea in a tidal wave that swept over everything on land, leaving death and destruction in its wake. The Vietnam War was raging, and angry crowds were demonstrating in the streets in protest against the war, and young men were fleeing to Canada to escape being drafted. The new president, Lyndon Johnson, was having a difficult time but stubbornly persisted in his war efforts, until finally he gave up and refused to run for a second term.

And in the election that followed, the assassinated president's younger brother, Robert, came back to political life and ran for the office, only to be gunned down in a San Francisco restaurant. There was no end to all the turmoil. Now it was the sixties, with freedom marches, sit-ins by blacks at restaurant counters demanding to be served just as white people were, and Martin Luther King, Jr. making his great speech in the huge Washington demonstration, "I have a dream . . ." Then he too was shot and killed, by a sniper hidden in bushes across the street from the motel where King was staying. Riots followed, with buildings set on fire by infuriated blacks.

The whole country, it seemed, was on fire. At the time all these things were happening our two children, no longer children now but a young man and young woman, were in college, Charlie at Boston University, Adraenne at Vassar.

One day I received a telephone call from a man I did not know. He gave me his name, but I had never heard it before.

"What is it you want?" I asked.

"I have a message from your daughter, Adraenne," he said.

"What do you mean, you have a message?" I said. "Can't she give me her message herself?"

"No, she can't," he said.

"Why not?"

"Because she's in jail."

I had to pause a minute to take this in. Then I said, "What the hell are you talking about?"

"She's been arrested along with a number of others. They were in the freedom march in Birmingham, Alabama, and police grabbed a number of them and put them in jail. I was in the march too, but I was lucky. They didn't arrest me. Adraenne asked me to get in touch with you and tell you what happened."

I was utterly bewildered at first. My daughter in a freedom march in Birmingham, Alabama, and now in a jail there when she was supposed to be at Vassar College attending classes?

"I don't get this," I said. "How'd she ever get involved with this business, and who are you, anyway?"

"Adraenne has been a member of the Vassar freedom fighters for some time, and she was in the Vassar contingent that came to the march. I'm a member too, and I'm a student at the University of Chicago."

So that was it. That was one of perhaps many other things she hadn't told us about. My kids were growing up, all right. I talked with Ruby about it, not knowing what to do next, and she saw no reason to get disturbed over it; she said she'd probably have done the same thing herself at her age if there had been such a thing as freedom marches. Just the same, she thought it would be a good idea to try to get her out of jail as soon as possible.

I called the Birmingham police department, and a gruff voice with a strong southern accent spoke to me. He was Sergeant somebody or other, but he knew all about the arrests of the freedom marchers and made it quite clear that he didn't like any of them. As for my daughter, if she was one of them, she deserved to be where she was, and if I was so concerned over her, why didn't I keep her home where she belonged instead of letting her come to another city and stir up trouble?

For a few moments, while all this was coming out of him, I could not get a word in, and his gruff voice went on nonstop.

Finally, I was able to say, "All I want is to know how I can get her out of there. If there's bail involved, I'll be glad to put it up."

"You better talk to your lawyer about that," he said. "As far as I'm concerned, she's gonna stay here forever."

It wasn't very encouraging, and Ruby began to feel worried. I did talk to my lawyer, and he in turn referred me to a lawyer who specialized in civil rights matters. Her name was Bella Abzug. I had never heard of her then, but she would be in the newspapers often in the coming years, in the forefront of the civil rights struggle, eventually elected to Congress, and famous for the wide-brimmed hats she wore. At the time she lived in a brownstone house in downtown Manhattan, and it was her office also. I went there to see her, a large woman with a harsh voice that had an East Side accent and a perpetual frown on her not very attractive face.

We spoke only for a few minutes in the crowded little room that was her office, with frequent interruptions of the telephone, and she promised to look into the matter and see what could be done to get my daughter released. Before I left she asked for a retainer of two hundred dollars. I wrote a check and left, feeling more uncertain and worried than when I had come.

"We might have to look for another lawyer," I said to Ruby. "I'm not sure about this woman."

But the next day Adraenne was released, and I'll never know whether it was through Bella Abzug's efforts or it would have happened anyway because the following day all the others who had been arrested were released. But Adraenne was out of jail, and we were relieved. However, it was quite clear to us from that day on that our children were no longer under our control. They were grown-ups, with minds and wishes of their own. As soon as Adraenne had graduated from Vassar, she no longer wanted to live at home, but made a home of her own, a dark little room in a tenement house on the Lower East Side of New York, among noise and filth. We knew little of her life and saw her only occasionally, and later on she moved to California to live in similar surroundings in San Francisco, and we saw her even less often then, until finally she returned to New York to live and become a nurse practitioner, and one day she introduced us to her husband. His name was Walter, and he played the trumpet, and occasionally got a gig with a band. He was about fifteen years older than Adraenne and had a beard that was beginning to show gray; he was African American, and had a good sense of humor and laughed often.

"It's what she wants," Ruby said, defending the choice our daughter had made, one that I did not particularly care for. "She's happy with him and that's all that matters."

As for Charles, he did not wait long to get married. Before graduating from Boston University he went out to Iowa to take a summer course in photojournalism, and he came back with Ruth and announced they were going to be married. We were stunned: He was too young, he hadn't even graduated from college yet. We weren't even sure we liked Ruth. She was from a small town in Iowa where her father owned a drugstore, and that part was all right, but she seemed cold and distant toward us. Probably this was due to the fact that she sensed our disapproval of the marriage. She stayed with us for a few days, then suddenly one day left, Charlie with her. They got married, and it made us realize even more how little we had to say about our children now.

But the marriage seemed to work out. Charles graduated and got a job on the staff of a McGraw-Hill trade magazine, and a year later Steven was born. So our family was growing. We now had a grandchild. Two more were added later, though these two were adoptions, a Korean girl named Susan and a little black girl from Harlem, Caroline. The marriage seemed to be lasting until Charlie met Ann at the firm where he then worked as a public relations manager, and soon he and Ruth were divorced and now we had a new daughter-in-law, and from this second marriage came two more grandchildren, Pete and Kate.

It took still another divorce and a third marriage and divorce before Charlie finally met Marcy, his fourth and last wife, in whom he found the soul mate he had been seeking, an attractive woman with a kind heart and a good sense of humor.

Throughout all this period of Adraenne's and Charlie's struggles to adjust to the uncertainties and difficulties of life and to achieve what is called settling down, Ruby and I experienced the only upsets in what otherwise could have been a perfect life. But it seemed to be all over finally, and we were now alone in our ugly brick bungalow that had served us so well during all these years.

We were in our sixties. My hair, what was left of it, was completely gray. Ruby's soft dark hair remained virtually untouched, and her face showed no signs of aging. Not to my eyes. We were as much in love with each other as ever, and perhaps now that we were alone together it was even stronger.

But I felt a need for change. By this time I was tired of editing Myron's skinny moneymaking magazines and having to listen to his domestic problems. I needed a rest from it all. I was now eligible for Social Security, and with both of us working we had managed to save some money over the years and Ruby would have a pension, all of which would enable us to live comfortably on a modest income if we retired.

When I brought the subject up to her she seemed unhappy about it. She liked her job; she would hate to give it up. I argued with her. I pointed out that we could sell our house and buy a new one in one of the retirement communities that were springing up everywhere these days.

But again she seemed troubled, and perhaps this was her major reason for not wanting to agree to my plan: the neighborhood was changing. Many of the old-time residents had left, and their homes had been bought largely by blacks; this was due to a great extent to the blockbusting tactics of Realtors who went from door to door among the old-timers urging them to sell their home before the influx of newcomers would bring real estate values down to nothing. Ruby resented it and refused to be frightened; I felt pretty much the same as she did, and it was for that reason we held out much longer than most people did, until finally we both agreed that retiring would be best for us, along with a change of environment: a new home, a new place, new friends, new everything. It began to seem more and more desirable, and finally we did it.

We sold our home to a young Haitian couple, who reminded us a little of ourselves when we were their age and bought our first home. They were a smiling couple with one child, and this would be their first home. As they went through the rooms looking here and there, awe and wonder showed on their faces. They saw no ugliness in its architecture, only beauty and probably the fulfillment of the dream we ourselves had once had when we lived in our furnished room.

Ruby and I felt glad we were turning our house over to them, and in the meanwhile we had been looking for a new place to live.

We had scoured all the so-called leisure villages, seeking the one we thought would be best for us. We even traveled to Florida to look at Century Village there, and were tempted by the thought of being able to escape the cold in the winters, but finally were discouraged by the barracks-like look of the house. We drove up to a place in Connecticut. It was built on sloping hilly ground, and the architecture here appealed to us considerably. All the houses were different from what we had seen before, and there was one model in particular that interested me. It had two floors, with the bedrooms upstairs, and I liked that particularly.

But Ruby had a more practical mind than I and saw things ahead that I failed to see. "Darling," she said, "don't you think you'll ever get old?"

I was puzzled. I couldn't see any reason for her asking that. "What's that got to do with the price of cheese?" I asked.

"A lot. When people get old they might have some difficulty climbing a flight of stairs every night to go to bed. And the terrain of this place is hilly, so if you want to take a walk and you're in your seventies or eighties—if we should live that long—you might have some trouble."

She was right. I'm glad now that I listened to her. The two of us lived well past our eighties, and walking was one of the things we enjoyed doing most; the place we finally chose to live in, Greenbriar, was in a flat area that made it easy to walk.

Greenbriar was in south-central New Jersey, and we were drawn there by the fact that the houses were all separate from one another and were on fairly large plots. Most of the others we had seen were in attached groups and had an institutional look to them. The Greenbriar houses varied in appearance and gave a feeling of individuality that we liked.

But what really made up our minds about buying a house there was the fact that all the streets were named after famous writers of the past, and when we were told there was one available on Dickinson Road—named after our favorite poet, Emily Dickinson—we grabbed it.

So there came a day at last when we locked the door of that ugly brick bungalow for the last time and got into our car to drive to the new home. As we left I could not help feeling a pang of regret. It had served us well in all the thirty-five years we had been there. We had done a lot of living in it. We had raised two children there, and a lot of pets—cats, dogs, chickens, hamsters (including the pregnant one that had only a short life in the lining of my car), parakeets, goldfish, and probably other creatures that I have forgotten.

As we drove off I caught a last glimpse of the piles of garbage in black bags that we had assembled after clearing out the attic, the basement, the garage, and all the drawers and cupboards, and again I could not help feeling a pang of something deep inside me. Those bags contained the memorabilia, the souvenirs, of all the years we had spent there: the first scribbled drawings of our children, the high school and college graduation programs for both of them, the concert and theater programs that Ruby always took home from the theater and stored endlessly in her dresser drawer, snapshots that had faded, maps that we had used in our travels, bills that were marked paid, pots and pans that we no longer needed or were worn out, and all sorts of things that we had stored for sentimental reasons but now were just garbage and would be taken away by the city garbage wagon and disposed of forever.

I had found it hard throwing them away. I hesitated over each one before putting it in the garbage bag. They seemed to have a rightful place with us and to still belong in our life. But I consoled myself, thinking that our old life was over and we were beginning a new one.

I think Ruby was feeling the same way I was. She too had glanced behind her as we drove off and had seen that mountainous pile of black bags. Her hand reached out and touched mine on the wheel, and I took it in mine and pressed it.

As we were driving away, I was still looking through the rearview mirror at the pile of garbage we had left behind, and I saw Mr. Way come hurrying out of his house, dressed in his World War I khaki uniform. He came to a halt and stood looking in our direction, standing at attention, then saluted us. I don't know if he saw me, but I saluted back to him, and it completed our departure.

Chapter Seventeen

2005

I'D HAD ONE OF MY BAD NIGHTS BEFORE THE CALL CAME. I HAD NOT been able to fall asleep and lay in the darkness thinking of all sorts of things of the past, some of which I had written about in my book, an assortment of episodes, faces, voices, little snatches of vignettes, all of them disconnected, passing fleetingly through my mind. Then I got to thinking of Ruby and a time shortly after we were married when we went on a walking tour through New England. We had joined an organization called the American Youth Hostel Association. They would map out an itinerary for you, and there were hostels in farmhouses where you could stay for twenty-five cents a night and get a meal there for very little money.

We had a gay time of it. We both loved walking, and we loved the hills and mountains that we went through, and we loved the hostels that we came to at night, even though they were sometimes beds in haylofts, the sweet smell of hay all around us. And we loved each other. There was a sweetness about all this that made me cling to the recollection for quite some time.

But then, suddenly, my thoughts made an ugly turn, and I began to think of what we had done to Ruby when she had died. She had wanted cremation, but neither she nor I had given any thought to what that really meant. It meant burning her, destroying her until there was nothing left but ashes, and horror came over me as I lay there thinking of it. How could I have turned her lovely body over to be thrust into an oven of flames?

But what else was there? Was burying her under the ground and letting her rot slowly away any less barbaric? But why think of either alternative? What difference did it make? She was gone, and that was all that mattered.

So once again I found myself back in the misery of wanting her, missing her, and crying for her, although perhaps it had never left me. The year I had spent writing my book had been temporary forgetfulness. I thought I had made things worse now by sending my book out to publishers and adding the bitter disappointment of failure. I berated myself that I should have known that would be the inevitable result. I had brought it on myself, and perhaps I deserved what I was getting now.

It was in this black mood that I got up next morning and began stumbling through making my breakfast. I had been clumsy before under ordinary circumstances, but now I was doubly so. Things fell out of my hands, toast burned, I knocked over a glass of orange juice, and I did a lot of cursing. I was in this state when the telephone rang.

On top of everything else! I stood with a mop in my hand, about to wipe up the spilled orange juice that covered half the kitchen floor, wondering who the hell could be calling me at this time of the morning. My daughter reminding me to take my pills? My son asking if I needed anything?

With one hand still holding the mop, I lifted the receiver of the phone with the other hand, put it to my ear, and said "Hello" in a voice that could not have sounded pleasant to the other party.

A woman's voice answered, "Is this the residence of Harry Bernstein?"

"Yes," I barked, deciding now that it was a saleswoman, and getting ready to bang the receiver down.

"Are you the author of *The Invisible Wall*?"

This was something else. I felt my heart give a jump.

"Yes," I said in a much more careful tone.

"I'm Kate Elton," the voice said, "an editor at Random House, and I'm calling from our office in London to tell you that I've read your book and I like it very much, and I'm prepared to make you an offer."

What could my reaction be to that? What could be the reaction of anyone who has spent his lifetime trying to write a book that would be published, and finally in his ninety-fifth year has succeeded in doing so? What came to me then was skepticism. Although my heart started beating violently, I became cautious. This was a young voice, and young people didn't make offers to publish books.

"Who did you say you were?" I asked.

"Kate Elton."

I will never forget that name. "Are you in authority there?"

"I am the editorial director of the Arrow Books division of Random House."

Could there be anything more authoritative than that? My heart was going rapidly now. All the skepticism had vanished. This was real. I didn't know what to say next. The voice went on to say that I would receive the offer shortly by mail, and this would be followed by a contract, which I should sign and send to them; she ended by telling me again how wonderful my book was and that Random House would be proud to be my publisher.

I hung up in a daze. I stood staring at the spilled orange juice on the floor. I began to mop it up, but it was no longer something I wanted to curse over. In fact, I was glad to have this task because it steadied my nerves a little.

It should not be hard to picture how I felt at this moment, how anyone would feel after a lifetime of trying and failing and then finally, when my life was virtually over, to find the success I had always been searching for. I remembered the time another editor had sent for me to discuss the novel I had submitted to him. The euphoria had been the same then as it was now, inspired by the certainty that he was going to accept my book, only to tell me he still had faith in me as a coming writer but that for the moment the answer was no. What a different outcome this talk with an editor had had now.

This thought led to thinking of Ruby, and how I wished she could have shared this moment with me. I had mostly kept my disappointments from her, if I could help it. But those that she knew about she dismissed lightly, telling me that they were unimportant and that I was bound to make it someday. She would not have been surprised had she been alive. But she would have been happy about it.

Adraenne was wildly happy when I relayed the news to her on my cell phone, finding her on a subway riding to the hospital where she worked. Charles took the news a bit more soberly but with equal, unmistakable joy in his tone. They'd both been brought up to the sound of my typewriter clattering away in the office I had in the house where we lived. When I'd had some time to spare, I lost none of it going down to this basement office, which was a table next to the oil burner, inserting a sheet of paper in the typewriter, and for the next few hours becoming oblivious of everything except the novel I was banging out at a rapid pace.

The news that I had finally achieved what I had sought all those years must have come as a shock to them, but nevertheless a wonderful surprise. It was to me. I had not expected it, but as I said, there was a shadow cast across that joy when I thought of Ruby and wished she could share it with me. I remembered only too well the terrible letdown I'd had in store for her the day I went to see Clifton Fadiman and he handed my manuscript back to me with such sad regrets. Ruby and I had expected to celebrate our dinner that night with even more fervor than we had the previous night, when it seemed so certain that I'd brought a bottle of wine to toast my success.

I remembered wondering how I was going to break the news to her, especially when I heard her footsteps hurrying up the stairs with such expectancy in them, and when the door opened her eyes went to me with that look in them, and her arms were already around my neck for a kiss of congratulations. I told her as we embraced, and it didn't change a thing. She laughed and hugged me still tighter.

"So what?" she said. "If it didn't happen today, it will happen some other time. But it's bound to happen. So let's drink a toast to that in advance, and we'll drink again when it happens."

There was wine left from the day before, and that's exactly what we did do. We filled our glasses and touched them, toasting to what was going to happen, and we kissed, and I never felt the disappointment and embarrassment that I had expected to feel.

Well, it had happened, just as she had said it would, and I de-

cided to do what she would have done. I put a fresh white lace table-
cloth on the dining room table that night and set the table for two. I
went out and bought a bouquet of flowers and a bottle, not of wine,
but of champagne. I placed the flowers in the center of the table
along with a framed photograph of her.

I had also bought a roast chicken in the supermarket, and it gave
off a delicious odor that mingled with the scent of the flowers. There
could not have been a more beautiful table. All it lacked was her
presence. But I had to make do with what there was. I sat down and
filled the two glasses with champagne. I raised mine and looked at
her photograph. She was smiling back at me.

"To you, darling," I said.

But my hand shook and I had to put the glass down; it was several moments before I could recover enough to drink or eat.

Chapter Eighteen

1973

GREENBRIAR WAS DESIGNED WITH A CIRCULAR SHAPE. SEEN FROM above in a plane, it would have resembled a huge wheel, with the clubhouse in the center as the hub and the streets radiating from it as the spokes. But I think the architect may have had a more profound thought. That circular shape could have meant another world, a world within a world that had been carved out of the surrounding pine forests, sheltered from the outside world by remaining thick clusters of pine trees that gave off their constant sharp, coniferous smell.

Perhaps, as I suspect, the architect might have been trying to say, *You are completely isolated from the world you have come from, with its noises and crime and pollution. Here you will be protected from all that in your golden years.* And as the promoters of the community would add, *Here you will find a taste of heaven before the real thing comes, and here is where you will find that every night is Saturday night.*

Well, it wasn't exactly like that, but it was quite definitely quiet and peaceful, and the surroundings were pleasant, and we had a comfortable house that gave us a view of the man-made lake around which every morning before breakfast Ruby and I would walk briskly, feeling younger and healthier than ever. The lawns were green and spacious, and in between the houses were broad stretches of common ground on which there were no houses, but only trees and bushes, and flowers everywhere. Then too, there was a nine-hole golf course, shuffleboard courts, of course, two swimming pools, and a clubhouse where you would find a constant round of activities, including painting and sculpting and ceramics.

What more could anyone want in his retirement days, when he or she was free of the workday routine of having to sit in an office for eight hours every day? Here we could get up in the morning when we pleased, go where we pleased, do what we pleased, or do nothing at all. We no longer had the children to worry about and to get to school in the morning, and all the problems that went with their growing up. There was nothing, absolutely nothing, to worry about, and there were new friends to make. To Ruby's great delight there was dancing of all kinds at the clubhouse: square dancing, round dancing, line dancing, ballroom dancing, folk dancing. Greenbriar was the dancingest place in the world.

Ruby loved dancing of all kinds, but folk dancing especially, chiefly because it had an international flavor, and she got me into it. I had resisted at first. I didn't mind the ballroom dancing on Saturday nights, but once Ruby had broken down my resistance and persuaded me to attend the weekly folk dances, I could never get over a feeling of embarrassment at holding hands with people on either

side of me and sometimes skipping or hopping or twirling. I felt
plain silly, but I did it, and stuck to it every week because I saw how
much pleasure it gave Ruby, the glow it brought to her cheeks, and
the sparkle in her big brown eyes.

I didn't mind the Saturday night dances at the clubhouse with a
live band playing. It was called café night. We sat at tables with about
half a dozen other people, some of them couples like us, some sin-
gles, widows or widowers in their sixties or seventies. Coffee and
cake were served. There was very little talk among them. Some of
them simply sat and stared at the crowd dancing and never danced
themselves. But Ruby and I did, and we broke away from them as
soon as possible to go on the dance floor. I had become fairly profi-
cient at it under Ruby's tutelage, and ever since that first night ages
ago when we had met at a dance, I had lost none of the pleasure of
holding her close to me and moving to the rhythm of the music with
her, and feeling the warmth and softness of her body under the palm
of my hand.

We had returned to our table one night after the dance was over,
and I still had my arm around Ruby's waist as we sat down next to
two women who had been watching us. One of them spoke to the
other, loud enough for us to hear, winking and saying, "I think we
have a romance here." She then turned to me and asked, "How long
have you two been married?"

"About forty years," I said.

They were both amazed. The other woman said, "I can't believe
it. We were watching you dance and we were sure you were newly-
weds, the way you were dancing so close together and the way you
keep looking at each other. We were sure it was a second marriage
for both of you."

We assured them it was our first marriage and a forty-year-old one, and we were both amused and flattered by their incredulity. I don't think we had realized until then how noticeable our feelings toward each other were to others. But it would always be that way. It was the one thing that would never change.

So many of the good things don't last. Those early days in Greenbriar are among them. They went by too fast. But while they lasted we felt we were living a new life. Everybody felt that way. The community was new. It had been started only two or three years before we arrived there. They were still building houses and more new people were coming in. There was a sort of pioneering spirit among us that drew everyone together, and all the activities were well attended if for no other reason than everyone wanted to meet still more friends.

Although people were beginning to break off into different groups, it hadn't taken us long to find out that so many of the people there knew nothing about the authors whose name was given to the street on which they lived. They had no idea who Emily Dickinson was, or Whitman, or Poe, or any of the others who were so precious to us. They were people who had never read a book, and so they were the people we shunned. We found our own group of book lovers and music lovers. There were Bruce Davenport, a former history professor at Hofstra College, and his wife, Martha, and of course Pete and Ann Warth, who were bird watchers as well and introduced us to the wonderful world of flying creatures. And the Milowskys, Nate and Esther, whose home on Collins Avenue was a gathering place for us because Nate had an extensive collection of Victor Red Seal classical records, with all the old favorites such as Caruso and Maud Powell and other great singers and musicians. The collection occupied one entire wall of their house in glass cases that reached from floor to ceiling.

They are all dead now, but those gatherings in the Milowskys' house, with all of us listening in deep silence, enthralled by the music we heard coming off those ancient records, are vivid in my mind, and very precious to me.

Eventually, those gatherings broadened into a classical music club, and there were so many people in it the meetings had to be held in the auditorium at the clubhouse, and it was there that Sarah, a talented pianist, performed for us, with her husband, Jake, a retired New York cop, turning the pages for her and beaming proudly as she played.

These were the good days that went by too fast and made us feel that we were indeed living in another world, a sanctuary shut off from the outer troublesome world. But even then, I recall, when the place was still new for all of us, this illusion was shattered one day, and some of the evil of the outer world managed to penetrate our sanctuary.

One morning a woman resident was found dead in the pine woods surrounding the community. She was a widow who lived alone in a house on Poe Avenue, and she had been strangled. Clearly, this was a case of murder, and immediately following the discovery the place was swarming with police. The place that was being touted by its promoters as "a taste of heaven before the real thing comes along" was now a place of terror.

It did not take them long to find the culprit, one of the workmen on a new house they were still building. He was a young black man. He and the woman had struck up a friendship while she was walking her dog one day, and she had invited him into her home. He came several times, and they would sit and drink beer and chat and perhaps, it was surmised, do more than that. One night they got into an argument after too much beer, and the young fellow lost his temper and there was a struggle and he killed her, then carried the body out into the woods and dumped it there.

Surprisingly, not much of this got into the papers, not even when the trial took place and the killer was sentenced to life imprisonment. I thought this might have had something to do with the fact that Greenbriar was a big advertiser in all the papers. I reasoned that it could well have halted sales if the public had been better informed about the murder. To me this looked like a cover-up, and a largely successful one at that.

Thinking about it, I felt there was something wrong in this. People were entitled to know the truth about a place in which they were going to live and that they were being told was another world of nothing but peace and harmony. The so-called leisure village was still something new, and not many people knew anything about them, so I decided that I would write an article and tell them what it was like living in one of these places. There was such a good story in Greenbriar that I simply could not resist writing it.

It was a long article, and I sent it off to the New York Sunday *News* magazine. It was accepted immediately, and the *News* made a big thing out of it. Their photographer spent three days out at Greenbriar taking pictures of the place and even went so far as to rent a plane and take aerial shots of the circular community. They made it their cover story, and the Sunday it appeared on the newsstands is one I will never forget.

Here in Greenbriar where the residents bought their newspapers, the *News* was soon sold out, and our telephone had not stopped ringing. There were calls from residents all over the place— and they were angry and abusive. They had found the entire article offensive, particularly the part that exposed the murder. They considered me a traitor and a troublemaker. It went on all day and night. There were midnight calls, anonymous voices uttering threats accompanied by profanity. It went on through the next day. Ruby answered one of the calls, which began with the F-word, only this time the caller was stupid enough to give his name. I reported it to the police, and they arrested the man, charging him with the use of profanity over the phone, a misdemeanor. However, I decided not to press charges after learning from him that he had not read the article but had only been told about it from some other residents. I gathered this was the case with many of them.

A special meeting of residents was called to discuss the matter, and it was broadcast over the community's closed-circuit TV. It ended with a statement that had been unanimously approved by the residents: "We believe that the Bernsteins would be happier living elsewhere."

Ruby was unhappy over the whole thing, perhaps even a little frightened. She thought perhaps we should move out. I refused to do so. On the whole, I don't think I minded the furor. It was a tribute to my writing. Nothing I had done before this had aroused such attention, and it was flattering to find people so stirred up by it. So we stayed, and after a while the whole thing died out and people began to talk to us again and it seemed to be forgotten.

In retrospect, I can see that I did a wise thing by sticking it out. I would never have forgiven myself if I had allowed them to drive us out. I had done nothing wrong. I had merely told the truth about a community and exploded a false myth of a heaven on earth. I had also won for myself the interest of the magazine's editor, and during the next year I wrote several more articles for him on a variety of subjects.

But that too died down, and the next years went by peacefully but all too swiftly. Suddenly, it seemed, we were in our seventies. Our friends were growing older with us, and one day we had the kind of telephone call that we were to receive often in the days ahead and that we dreaded. This one was from Nate Milowsky telling us that Esther had died during the night.

It was our first funeral of Greenbriar friends. It was sad. But sadder yet was the way in the months that followed how Nate tried to make us feel that nothing had changed and the music group still existed. We were all invited to his house as we always had been to listen to his Victor Red Seal records, to hear Caruso sing and Maud Powell and Fritz Kreisler and Mischa Elman play the violin. The music was just as wonderful as it had always been. But it was not the same as before.

When the time came to serve the refreshments Nate insisted on doing it alone, though there were plenty of volunteers who gladly would have done it for him. He brushed them aside and became angry when they insisted. He spilled milk on the table, the coffee was terrible, the cake he tried to cut fell apart. But no, he must do it all himself.

I visited his house several times during this period. Ruby urged me to go because she could not bear the thought of his being alone so much. I hated to go because the house smelled and he always had the windows closed even in the warmest weather, and they were so dirty you could not see through them. The rest of the house was never cleaned either, and the smell grew worse every time I went. Then, finally, there was no reason to go. Nate had not been seen for three days, and when people knocked on the door there was no answer. The police were called, and when they broke into the house they found Nate lying on the floor, dead. He had been dead for three days. There was one of his Victor Red Seal records in the player and it was still twirling, though silent, having reached the end, with the automatic stop apparently having failed to work. The record was of Caruso singing Verdi's "Fontainebleau, foresta immense" from *Don Carlos*. How much of it Nate heard I'll never know.

Pete Warth was the next one in our group to go. He suffered a stroke and lay in a coma for weeks, and during that time I drove Ann to see him every day since she herself did not drive. I watched her as she went up to the snoring figure in the bed, bent over him, and spoke to him as though he were conscious and aware of her presence, saying, "How are you today, Pete? This is your wife, Ann, and Harry is with me, and we've both come to visit you. Is there anything you need? Tell me, I'll get you anything you want. Would you like some pickled herring?"

She kept that up day after day, and with it there came a withdrawal from us, from everybody. She began to speak to us as if she did not know us. She spoke strangely of things we did not understand. The only time she seemed coherent was when she was talking to Pete. Then he died, and her son, a doctor in Boston, came and took her away. When we called once to find out how she was, she could not speak to us, and the son told us she no longer knew us or any of the others she had lived among. She too died in a short time.

Perhaps the death and the funeral that was held that shocked us more than any of them was the one of Phil Frazer, another member of the music group, but a still vigorous and athletic man well into his seventies. He had been a football coach at a high school and still retained his athletic ability, especially in tennis. He played often. Almost every day during the summer you could see him striding off to the tennis court clad in his white shorts and shirts, carrying a tennis racket.

His wife, Sylvia, didn't play and was nowhere near being athletic. She looked every bit of her age. One day, we learned later from others, she'd begged him not to go to the tennis courts. It was a hot day in July and she felt he ought to stay home with her. He refused and went off with his racket, dressed in white, smart-looking, his hair white too, but making him look all the more handsome, and in the middle of the game he dropped dead on the tennis court from a heart attack.

It was the funeral that shocked us. The ceremony was held at a nearby funeral parlor—the one that had a full-page advertisement in the *Greenbriar Times*—and Sylvia was crying bitterly throughout the ceremony. In the midst of it she rose and screamed at the coffin: "So, you had to go and play tennis! I told you not to go! I begged you! But you wouldn't listen! And now look at you. What did you get from your tennis and your fancy white clothes? You couldn't stay home for once? And now what am I to do? What's to become of me? Oh, Phil, you fool, you fool!"

Somehow they got through with the ceremony and the burial and the rebuke that she kept up to the very end.

The deaths came one after the other, like leaves dropping off the trees in the autumn, leaving bare skeletons of trunks and branches. The men nearly always went first. There were whole streets where the houses were occupied by widows. Our music group went one by one until there was no one left to listen or to perform except Ruby and myself. We lived, the two of us, among strangers, the new people who had come in to take the places of the ones who had gone, new people who seemed very young to us, who were as young as we had been when we first came here, young in spirit looking forward to the best years of their lives, and never suspecting how short those years would be.

And yet Ruby and I did not feel lonely among them. We still enjoyed our life because we were together, both of us well and still able
to walk around the lake—less briskly, to be sure, as we entered our
eighties, but we could walk nevertheless, and we could still drive the
car and go places. In fact, we bought a new car in 1994. It was an
Oldsmobile, a Cutlass four-door.

But if we did not go on long cross-country drives by car, we
went to distant places by plane. We went to Mexico every winter to
bask in its warmth and sun for three months. It had become a second home to us, the little colonial town of San Miguel de Allende,
where the narrow cobbled streets rose until they reached their full
height, from which point you could look down and see the entire
town, with the tall steeple of the *parroquia,* the town's most ancient
church, dominating the view.

We loved this place and we could always look forward to a
warm welcome from Mucia, the little dark woman who owned
the Hotel Quinta Loreto, where we stayed every year, and then for
the next three months we would be well fed with her sumptuous
meals, well entertained with all the concerts and lectures and art
shows that took place in that town, or spend pleasant hours simply
sitting in the *jardin* bathed in sunshine or talking to other Americans.

Ruby and I passed from our eighties into our nineties never
dreaming that all this would be over someday and we would be separated. I think we were closer than ever during those late years, and
despite the fact that we had lost not only friends but family members too, we had the comfort of each other to make us feel that we
were still part of the world.

Ruby's mother had died a long time ago, not long after we had

been married, in fact, and it had been a terrible loss to Ruby, sending her into a deep depression that had lasted for weeks. When her
brother died some years later, she was without family altogether, except for mine.

But then mine too began to go. My mother was the first, her
dream of a wonderful America ending one bitterly cold day in a
dark basement flat in the Bronx. As for my father, he remarried
twice after that and died peacefully in his sleep one night. My oldest brother, Joe, was the first among us in America to die, at a relatively young age from cancer of the pancreas, and Rose was next,
only then finally giving up her pretense of being an aristocratic
Englishwoman, succumbing also to cancer in a hospital. Her husband, Jim, whom we all loved for his good nature, had died a short
time before her. Then Saul was next to go, and Sidney, the youngest
of us all, suffered a stroke and died in his eighties. Thus Lily, the
oldest, had been the first of us to die, years ago in England. I was the
sole survivor of all my brothers and sisters and my mother, whom I
cared for so much.

So we were alone, just the two of us, finally. To be sure, there
were our children and grandchildren; they had not forgotten us, and
they came to visit whenever it was possible. But my son lived in
Pennsylvania, Adraenne in Brooklyn, both seventy-five miles away,
and we did not see them as often as we would have liked.

Just the same, Ruby and I never felt alone being together, and we
were still mobile, still well enough to go places, doing things, enjoying life. Ruby continued to teach her yoga class at the clubhouse
every Wednesday morning until she was past ninety-one, and I
never ceased to marvel at the slenderness and shapeliness of her figure in her leotard. It lasted until that fateful morning in September

when we were in Ruby's room at the hospital and I was standing at the window looking across the street at Central Park and thinking of the days when Ruby and I had spent so much of our time there during our courtship, and suddenly I heard my daughter cry out, "Dad, she's stopped breathing. She's dead!"

Chapter Nineteen

2006

WHEN I HEARD KATE ELTON'S VOICE OVER THE TELEPHONE SAY, "I'VE
read your book and I like it very much, and I'm prepared to make
you an offer," a whole new life began for me in my ninety-fifth year.
It was a bit like an explosion of fireworks on July 4, one burst after
another lighting up the sky in a brilliant display of colors. I felt the
same sort of thrill as I would have watching that take place. I had my
imaginary celebration dinner with Ruby. I know it sounds foolish,
but it was a time to do foolish things. I only wished some of my
friends were alive also, especially the ones who had viewed my writing efforts with a certain amused skepticism. The admiration, the
awe, and, yes, the envy from the people who know you is part of the
reward of being an author.

The truth is, I didn't quite know what to do after receiving that
message from Kate Elton, whom I would always regard with deep

gratitude as the one editor out of a thousand who had found my book good enough to be published, and in doing so had made the last years of my life the most productive and exciting of my entire lifetime.

I wished I could walk, so that I could walk off some of the exhilaration that I felt. But my ability to walk had lessened still further, and about the best I could get out of any doctor was "learn to live with it." Or did he mean "die with it"? But there was nothing obvious that could be done save make sure that I protected myself from falls and used a cane or a walker.

I contented myself with being able to make my way across the street to the lake, leaning on my walker, and sit on the bench that Ruby and I used to rest on after our walk around the lake, and in the evenings watch the sun set on the other side of the lake. It was quiet and restful. It calmed me down.

I thought of her then as I had done so often before, but with even deeper longing than ever, and with such wishful thinking that I began to create fantasies in my mind. I imagined that what was happening now, with my book, had instead happened in the early days, even before our marriage, in the days of our golden willow— our golden boudoir, the lovely tree that had given us sanctuary and such peace and happiness. And I was terribly sorry once again that the one we'd had in our own garden was gone. But the memory was still there, especially of the first one in Central Park and the night we had slipped away from the concert on the mall to discover it, and the days and nights that had followed.

My wishful thinking, my fantasies, were about all of that, and I would picture myself walking into Brentano's bookstore, where Ruby worked, and saying to her quietly, "Can you take the day off?"

She looked bewildered. "Why?"

"I have something very important to tell you."

"Can't you tell me now?"

"No, I'd rather get out of here first."

"I can't. We're very busy."

"Then quit the goddamn job." How often had I said that in my imagination? How often had I argued in there and pulled her by the arm and told her she was quitting the goddamn job?

She stared at me. "Darling," she whispered, frightened a little, "what's the matter? What's happened?"   ·

"What's happened," I would say next, "is that I'm going to have a book published."

And she would stare at me, her mouth open a little, not quite believing what I had said. And then gradually it would register with her, and her expression became transformed into one of great joy and she would throw her arms around my neck and kiss me, with all the other employees and some customers staring at us.

Yes, I'd gone through that fantasy many times before, dreaming of having a book published and becoming a famous author, seeing my book displayed in bookstore windows, being interviewed by reporters, being asked for my autograph.

What wonderful things dreams are! They can make you be anything you want and take you anyplace in the world. And some of them can actually come true, as this one had for me. In the meantime, I sat on that bench near the lake wishing it had all taken place in the past, and creating fantasies about how my book was published when we were still living in one of Madame Janeski's furnished rooms on West 68th Street, and how my book enabled us to move into a fantastic big apartment, a penthouse with a view of the Manhattan skyline, not the two-room place on Bleecker Street that we did finally move into after I got my job as a reader for a moving picture company.

How wonderful all that would have been for us then, when we were both young and able to appreciate all the exciting things that can happen to a famous author. Well, it was too late now. Ruby was gone and I was alone. Yet there was a lot in store for me that I had missed before but could still appreciate and enjoy.

But first, before all this could happen, there was the book to get published, and it did not take me long to discover that there was more to publishing a book than simply writing one. My editor was Anna Simpson, a young woman with a gentle voice that came often over the telephone, but sharp eyes that ferreted out every little mistake in spelling, punctuation, grammar, or inconsistencies in the story that I had not been aware of. Revisions had to be made, proofs corrected, book jackets to be approved, bios and condensations of the book to be written for the publicity department.

I was kept busy with the various communications—e-mail, regular mail, FedEx, telephone—and I delighted in all of it. Nor did I mind going back over a book that I had already spent more than a year writing in order to correct the proofs.

Yes, there was a good deal more work than I had expected, but it was all pleasurable work, and for the first time in my life I felt what it was like to be a published author. My ego swelled further when I learned that photos of my family were to be used to illustrate the book. I had dug into albums and boxes where photographs had been stored from the days in England, and came up with a gem that showed my mother and the children in the family gathered around her with me an infant sitting on her lap. It had been taken in front of the house where we lived, on the street that I had written about. It was a picture that would be seen often, not only on the jacket of the book but in the reviews and articles that would be written later and published in newspapers.

Some inkling of the interest in my book had already been generated at the London book fair, where *The Invisible Wall* had been introduced, and to add to all my joy several foreign publishers had bought rights to publish in their countries. This was a totally unexpected bonanza. I'd had no idea that you could sell your book to more than one publisher, and it meant money that was badly needed.

I was two years older than when I'd first started writing my book, and my physical condition, though considered quite good for someone my age, had deteriorated to a point where I was having more and more difficulty getting around. I could not walk now without the aid of a walker, and I was finding it almost impossible to take care of myself. I needed someone to cook my meals, to shop for me, to do my laundry. My daughter came once every two weeks and did what she could to help me out, but she was too tied down to her job as a nurse practitioner and her own household to do more. My son also had little time to spare, and so I was alone most of the time, and I struggled to keep alive. Occasionally in trying to do some household work, I stumbled and fell and hurt myself, often badly.

Hospital emergency rooms are filled with elderly people brought in bleeding or with fractured bones resulting from their falls. I was lucky. I had several visits to the emergency room of our local hospital, but always with minor cuts and bruises. How long that luck was going to last was questionable. I was badly in need of a caregiver in my home, but I was unable to afford one until my book was sold to foreign publishers. The money came as an advance long before any

royalties were paid to me, and nothing could have been more welcome. And with it came Bette.

I saw her ad in a small newspaper that was thrust into my mail-
box once a month. It was in "Situations Wanted" and offered health
care services. I answered it immediately, and very soon the woman I
had spoken to arrived, and when I saw her for the first time it was
with a shock. Her face was swollen and a mass of scars. One of her
eyes seemed to be missing. She was about fifty, heavy and dressed in
ski pants and a jacket. The one good eye looked back at me defiantly,
as if aware of my reaction and daring me to remark on it.

I got over it in a moment and said, "Come on in and sit down
and let's talk."

Her first name was Bette and the rest of it was Italian. She told
me everything about herself. Several years ago she had been sitting
down to breakfast with her husband when they got into an argument over some trivial matter that she didn't want to talk about. It
was one of the few times they'd ever argued. Ordinarily, he was a
quiet, well-behaved man, a mechanic of some sort. He was her second husband and a good father to the two children, a boy and a girl,
she'd had with her first husband, whom she had divorced. But that
morning something happened to him and he went wild, and before
she knew it he was slashing at her face with a knife.

He ran off, leaving her unconscious and bleeding on the floor.
Eventually, they caught him and put him in prison with a fifteen-
year sentence. She herself spent months in the hospital, and it would
take months more of plastic surgery for her face to become normal
again.

In the meantime, she had been having difficulty finding work to
support her children, both of whom were still in school. She had

been a secretary before all this took place, but her disfigurement prevented her from getting a job. She tried everything, even the most
menial kind of work that was available, but prospective employers
shrank from her appearance. She told me all this quite calmly. There
was nothing emotional about her. In fact, she seemed almost amused
at her plight. But I couldn't help being touched by it, and somehow I
couldn't help feeling that we had something in common. Wasn't age
a disfigurement to many people? Age, with its bent figure, wrinkled
face, and crippled crawling movements, turned people off. I had seen
it in faces that looked at me.

I was more fortunate than others. I had written a book and gotten it published. But that didn't make any difference to the eyes that
looked at me. I was an old man, and I remember how I myself used
to feel when I was young and looked at old people. It was in the days
when I still lived in England, and there was Old Biddy, as we used to
call her and whom we dreaded meeting on our way through Daw
Bank, one of the more run-down sections, where the middens were
in front of the hovels there and overflowed onto the sidewalk. Old
Biddy would come out of one of the hovels looking like a bear that
had just been aroused from its winter hibernation, a slightly dazed
look on her wrinkled face but the eyes glaring at us fiercely, the voice
muttering something indistinct. We believed she was a witch, and
we ran from her in terror.

Any old person could arouse such fear in us, for we believed they
were all witches, some with toothless, grinning faces who could easily cast a spell on us. But there was one I recall for whom we felt pity.
This was old Bubba Frank, as she was called, *bubba* meaning "grand-
mother." She was bent over almost double—like a hairpin—with
what was undoubtedly osteoporosis, still unknown to the medical
world. She came often into my mother's faded fruit and vegetable

shop to pass the time, to sit with the other women and gossip while they sat around the counter and sipped the glasses of sour milk that my mother made and sold at a farthing a glass. She talked about herself and often wept over the misery of her life. Her care was being divided between two married daughters, the Blanks and the Londons, and the two sisters often quarreled over whose turn it was, neither one wanting her and each accusing the other of cheating on her turn. It was a common sight to see one of the daughters leading the old woman determinedly to the house of the other and then to hear them arguing on the doorstep while the old woman stood helplessly at one side waiting for the outcome of the argument and to know where she would be living for the next month.

Now I have overcome much of the prejudice directed at older people by writing a book, but I also have detected a note of skepticism in some people's voices, as if they might suspect that a doddering old man like me could well have made it up. I have noticed even slight amusement on others' faces, as if the idea of a ninety-plus-year-old man writing a book was akin to some sort of a circus stunt.

Nevertheless, I was an author and my book was in the process of being published, regardless of what anyone thought, and even before the publication date came about I was thinking of a second book that I would write, a sequel to the first one. But I pushed that aside for the time being, discouraged by the agent I had acquired in London. When I told him about the second book and had asked if he'd like to see an outline, he'd written back, "No, thanks. Be satisfied with what you've got, and remember, it isn't often that a publisher will take a chance on a first book by an author in his nineties."

I thought perhaps he was right; perhaps I was getting a bit too big for my britches. One day I heard the doorbell ring. I went to answer it. A FedEx deliveryman stood there with a large package in his hand. I took it from him, signed a sheet of paper, and took the package in. When I opened it I was staring at my first published book, ten of them neatly packaged. I took one off the top of the pile and held it before me, looking at it the way you would a newborn child—with awe, with joy. The cover, a greenish color, read:

THE

INVISIBLE

WALL

Harry Bernstein

There was a picture of a ragged young boy, who might have been me but wasn't, standing in front of a brick wall on a street a bit like mine. Turning to the back of the dust jacket, I saw a picture of my family in England, in front of the house where we had lived. My mother was in the center with me, about two years old, on her lap. To her left was my sister Rose on one side and Lily on the other. In front of them were Saul and Joe, my brothers.

I opened the back cover. There on the back inside flap was the author—me. It was a snapshot that my son had taken of me when I was visiting his summer home in Cape May.

I held the book in front of me and gloated. It was similar to the way I'd felt when I sold my first story to *The Chicagoan*. I was about seventeen, still in high school, and the check they had sent me with the acceptance was for ten dollars. I'd held that check up in front of me then the way I was doing with the book. It would take another eighty years before that same euphoria came back. But this time there would be a whole lot more to add to it.

Chapter Twenty

THE WORLD IN WHICH I WAS LIVING WHEN THE BOOK WAS PUB-
lished was vastly different from the one that I had written about. It
was, after all, nearly a hundred years later. Advances had been made
in every field—science, medicine, industry, transportation. We were
enjoying greater material comforts in life, and we were experiencing
greater longevity, so people like myself could be in their nineties and
still function in as normal a fashion as young people, and even write
books. But there were some things that hadn't changed, and one of
them was human nature and the wars that it brought on.

A war was raging now in, of all places, Afghanistan and Iraq,
with American troops combined with token British troops fighting
there for reasons that were not quite clear. Regardless, the fierce ac-
tion and the casualties that kept mounting higher each day filled the
newspapers and the TV screens, exciting everyone's attention and

occupying their minds, so I wondered what chance I had to distract them from all this with a book about a little cobbled street in the north of England where Jews lived on one side and Christians on the other, and all the things that happened there while I was growing up.

It looked as if there was little chance of my book getting any attention, and yet it did. It received a starred review in *Publishers Weekly*, and it got excellent reviews in all the leading papers in both England and the United States. The reception was just as enthusiastic in the various foreign countries where it had also been published—Norway, Sweden, Finland, Germany, Italy.

I was elated. I couldn't have been happier, especially when the *New York Times* published my picture on the front page. It showed me sprawled out in my reclining chair with a wide grin on my face. A *New York Times* photographer had taken it when he came with a reporter for an interview. It was one of many pictures to be taken and one of many interviews that followed in the weeks after publication. They came from abroad, too, from England, Norway, Sweden, Germany, and Italy, the last accompanied by a television crew. My phone rang often, and I gave interviews over the phone as well as at my house. At one time, when I was being interviewed by *USA Today*, a telephone call came from the London *Times*. They wanted an interview right then and there, and so I conducted two interviews at one time. And I received calls often from Sarina Evan, my publicist at Random House, asking if I would be available for this or that, perhaps a book signing, or a talk somewhere.

I gave my time willingly and gladly. This was something I might have dreamed about or fantasized over. It wasn't quite real, but I loved every moment of it. I was never so flattered as when I was asked to give a talk at the 92nd Street Y. I had been there often when I lived in New York to hear some truly great literary figures speak, such as Robert Frost, Carl Sandburg, and others, and to be asked to speak from the same platform as they had was the height of any ambition I might have had.

Obviously, there was as much interest in the author as in the book, and that isn't surprising. How often was it that a ninety-six-year-old man made his debut as a writer? I was, to be sure, an oddity, and Sarina made the most of it for Random House, landing me on the *CBS Evening News* and coming close to getting me on *Tonight* with Jay Leno.

I messed that one up myself. I rarely look at TV and had never even heard of this particular show or its star host, so when a woman called asking if I'd be interested in coming out to California and being on the show, I said, "What kind of show is that? And who is Jay Leno?"

There was a long pause. I imagine there was quite a shock at the other end of the wire, and then her voice came again, saying quietly, "Are you serious?"

"Yes, of course I am," I said. "And as far as traveling out to California goes, I'm afraid I can't travel, and if this Jay Leno wants to talk to me, he'll have to come out here."

I guess that did it. She promised to call back later and talk further, but I never heard from her again, and the invitation was never repeated.

Just the same, the book itself did not suffer from lack of attention, and in fact received wide acclaim from reviewers in newspapers all over the United States, England, and the various foreign countries where it was published. The *Daily Mail* of England said it was "a compelling narrative of childhood survival . . . the tale has a freshness, a vitality and a relentless energy . . . extraordinarily powerful . . . a triumph of the human spirit over multifaceted adversity."

What more could any writer ask for? And the *New York Times:* "A heart-wrenching memoir ... brilliantly illuminates a family struggling valiantly to beat impossible odds."

The Guardian called it "an exceptional book."

The book did not reach the best-seller list, but it was undoubtedly a literary success, and I had good reason to be proud of it. But occasionally a shadow was cast over all that as I realized that if Ruby had not died I would not have written the book or anything else.

I thought of that often and it hurt badly, and I tried to talk myself into believing that perhaps I was wrong and I might have written it anyway even if she had lived. Who knows, really, what men and women could be capable of in their nineties, what potential lies there in all of us? There are so few who live to such an age that it will not be possible to know until the limits of longevity are stretched much further than they are today and new medical knowledge enables us to go on even past the nineties and into our hundreds.

Chapter Twenty-one

2008

I LIVE ALONE NOW, BUT I AM NOT REALLY ALONE. MY MIND IS FILLED with the people I have been writing about for almost five years. Now that this, my third book, is completed, I have told the full story of my life from the time I was born, almost, until the time I will have died, again almost. I am now close to one hundred years old, so my guess can't be far off.

My second book, *The Dream*, was published a year after *The Invisible Wall*. This, probably my final book, is called *The Golden Willow* because that beautiful tree expresses the love that Ruby and I had for each other. As you have seen, it is about the period when both Ruby and I reached our nineties together, and it looks back on the wonderful sixty-seven years of marriage we had. It tells also of how I carried on alone, and what it is like to be in your nineties with all its loneliness and difficulties and physical impairments, but none of this without the hope and surprises that the nonagenarian years can bring—in my case, fulfilling a lifelong ambition to become an author, to write books that have won acclaim in the United States, England, and many other countries.

I feel a deep satisfaction in having accomplished all of this. It compensates a good deal for the loneliness I have felt, the sense of abandonment that came with being the sole survivor of all the members of my family, of all my friends and relatives, and especially of my wife.

I have finally experienced that touch of glory that I always yearned for, that perhaps everyone does, and at no time in all these last surprising years of mine, when all I had expected was to live out the last few years of my life comfortably and peacefully, was I so gratified as when I began to receive awards for my books.

The one that pleased me most was the Christopher Award. It was given to me for the spiritual content of *The Invisible Wall.*

I have often been asked during interviews how I compare the world of today to that of the one in which I was born, nearly a hundred years ago. I could not think of a better example of how it has changed than this moment when I received the Christopher Award at a reception in New York.

The Invisible Wall told of the small, cobbled street on which I was born and lived for twelve years, a street that was divided into two distinct parts by an invisible wall, with Jews living on one side and Christians on the other; rarely was there any crossing from one side to the other, or even any talking between people who lived on different sides. But here I was now, a Jew, receiving a plaque of honor from a Christian, a priest no less, together with a warm handshake, and there was the large audience rising to its feet to give me a standing ovation.

Yes indeed, there have been many changes.

Can there be a better example of change in the world than a black man becoming president of the United States, a man who in my world of a hundred years ago would not even have been allowed to vote in certain parts of the country, and would have been subject to all kinds of humiliations and degradations? I tell my interviewers that I have seen a lot of changes for the better take place in the world of today, both materially and spiritually, and I have a great deal of hope that they will continue to do so.

Our street in Lancashire no longer exists, and that is another big step forward in the new world. Ruby and I went there to see the place in the summer of 1960, and as I've noted, we arrived just in time to see it being torn down to make way for a public housing project that would eliminate such things as walls and bring all people to live together, side by side.

MOST OF THE TIME, however, when I am lying in bed unable to sleep, I am thinking of Ruby, and the wonderful years we had together. It is now almost seven years since she died, and despite the fact that my mind has been occupied with my writing, thoughts about her constantly have intruded, and the longing for her is as deep as it ever was. Counselors and authorities on the subject of grief say that time is the best healer, but time has done nothing for me. I do not feel any lessening of the grief now than I felt on that September morning when Ruby died.

No matter how busy I have been with my writing, she is always there with me still. I have never let go of her. I have her pictures all over the house, so I can see her no matter what room I am in. Her toothbrush is still in the bathroom. Her clothes still hang in the closet. Her shoes are there in the rack on the back of the closet door.

People tell me I am being foolish. They say I should dispose of these things, give her clothes to some charity organization and let some poor person make use of them, and all that will help me forget what has happened. I realize that is perhaps the rational thing to do, and yet I cannot bring myself to do it. I am afraid that I would lose her altogether, and so I cling to them along with the memories that keep her presence alive.

Among all the things that go through my mind on those nights when I lie awake are the regrets for things I have said and done that I know now were wrong, and I wish I could correct them. One of the things that bothered me a great deal was the time Ruby and I woke up after the thunderstorm to find our golden willow struck by lightning and lying uprooted on the ground in a shambles of golden leaves and branches.

I lay awake several nights thinking of this and remembering how Ruby wept over its loss. That tree meant a great deal to us. We had planted it ourselves, and we had watched it grow over the years with as much pleasure as we'd had watching our children grow. But the thing that troubled me most was that Ruby had asked if we couldn't plant another in its place, and I had said no, there wasn't enough time left for us to see it grow into maturity. She was silent afterward.

Why had I said that? It was the truth, yes, but did I have to remind her of it, and of her own mortality? That was probably what accounted for her silence. She probably sensed things about her illness that we didn't know. The anemia was not getting any better, and she required blood transfusions more and more often. I used to go with her to the hospital for them, and I would sit by her bed while the bag of red blood cells emptied slowly through the IV into her veins. She would read and I would read during the hours it took, and we would have lunch there and make a picnic out of it, and during all this time she maintained her cheerful manner, as if it were nothing at all. But I know now there were thoughts going on inside her that we knew nothing about, and my refusal that day to plant another tree had only added to those thoughts.

I allowed myself to be tormented with regret over all this for several nights. I couldn't stop thinking of how my remark must have struck deeply inside her and how stupidly insensitive I had been. What would have been wrong with going along with her and saying we'd plant another tree to take the place of the one that had died?

Then suddenly it occurred to me that I could make up for it, to some extent, by actually planting another golden willow. So what if she could not have lived to see it grow to maturity? So what if I didn't live that long?

I decided that it would at least ease my conscience by planting a golden willow now to take the place of the one that had been struck by lightning. It would also serve as a memorial to her, and to the two of us after I was gone. I was still turning that over in my mind when a remarkable coincidence took place the following morning.

I was at breakfast when the doorbell rang. I got up from the table, took hold of my walker, and went to the door. Two workmen from the community maintenance crew were there, and as if they had been reading my mind while I was in bed last night, one of them said, "Where do you want us to plant the tree?"

I stared at them stupidly, openmouthed. "What tree?" I asked.

The same one, who was obviously in charge, explained that it had been decided to replace all trees destroyed in a storm during the past few years, and my tree was on the list.

Of course, once I got over the shock of this remarkable coincidence I was overjoyed. I took them over to the garden and pointed out the place where our golden willow had once stood. "Right there," I said.

I watched as they went to their truck and took out one of the trees that were piled there. It was a thin, young sapling, much like the one we had planted years ago, but as I watched them dig the hole and then start to put the young tree into it I knew that there was something wrong. This wasn't a golden willow.

I grabbed my walker again and hobbled over to them. "Wait a minute," I said. "What kind of tree is that?" I spoke to both, and it was the one in charge who answered.

"Ornamental pear," he said, "like all the others we're putting in."

"Mine was a golden willow," I said. "That's what I should be getting if they're replacing the ones that were hit."

"Sorry," he said, "there's only one kind we're giving to everybody, and that's the ornamental pear. Anyway, they don't allow willows no more."

"Why not?" I asked.

"They're water grabbers. Their roots go for water wherever they are, and they've been damaging the underground water pipes we use for the sprinkling system, and damaging them so bad we gotta keep replacing them. So they put a ban on all willows."

I stared at him, aghast. What kind of crap was this? Whoever heard of putting a ban on willows, golden willows especially, the most beautiful of all trees? Perhaps the true reason was that golden willows cost more than other trees. I said this, but he shook his head and said he was only carrying out orders, and I could take it up with the trustees if I wanted.

I let the ornamental pear stay where they'd planted it, and I went back into the house fuming. I knew one of the trustees, and I called him up on the phone and told him what had happened. He said he was sorry, but the gardener was right. They were giving out just one kind, and it was absolutely true about the ban on willows because of the damage they'd done to the sprinkler system. However, there was one way out of it for me. I could buy a golden willow myself and they'd let me plant it on the lawn at the side of the lake where there was no sprinkling system.

I thanked him. This was a good idea, and the lawn at the side of the lake appealed to me. This was where Ruby and I used to sit on a bench on summer evenings and watch the sun set on the other side of the lake, the whole world turning pink and our faces bathed in its color. It would sink slowly bit by bit and the trees would turn dark with patches of that pink color showing through the branches, and it was always very quiet, with only the faint sound of birds bedding down for the night breaking the silence.

We had already planted a tree there, a London plane, as a memorial to Esther and her husband, Nate, when they had died. It had grown huge and its branches shaded the bench in the hot afternoons. Our golden willow would be just right there and would make a memorial park out of the spot.

But as soon as I began to look for my golden willow I ran into trouble. There were none. I called several nurseries and was told they were no longer carrying them. Evidently, other communities had experienced the same thing with their sprinkler systems, and the ban had spread. But the more difficult it became the more determined I was to find one. Finally I hit on a nursery in upper New Jersey that had several in stock. I lost no time buying one, and it was planted at the side of the lake directly facing the bench.

I felt satisfied. I only wished I had done it sooner, when Ruby was alive, but this was better than nothing. It was very young and frail. I had planted it at the wrong time. It should have been in the fall, when the cool weather would have helped it take root. But I had been in such a hurry to get this thing done that I had paid no attention to the weather. It was midsummer, and the young tree struggled in the blazing heat to stay alive. I had kind volunteer neighbors who carried buckets of water over to the tree to save it from dying. Loreen led the bucket brigade. She lived nearby. Every morning she could be seen walking her dog, carrying the leash in one hand, a bucket of water in the other. She knew the significance of the golden willow. She and the others succeeded. The tree lived on, showing tiny green leaves at the top of its thin branches.

It would grow. I felt confident of that. I would not be there when it reached its full maturity and it would blossom out into the shape of an old-fashioned ballroom gown, flowing gracefully downward with its branches trailing along the ground.

My not being there would make no difference. Its beauty would shine on for others to see, and that would be enough. I think I felt more satisfaction in having created this little memorial park than anything else I had created since I turned ninety.

During those evenings when Ruby and I sat watching the sunset, we'd sometimes talk about the early days. We had met one hot summer night at a dance, and I had taken her home to where she lived in Brooklyn; then I had walked all the way home that night to where I lived with my parents in the Bronx, miles and miles away, but hardly noticing the distance, so giddy I was with our meeting.

I couldn't wait for a respectable length of time to pass before I saw her again. I had to see her again on Monday, just two days later, which was as soon as she could manage. I arranged to meet her after she got out of Brentano's bookstore, where she worked. We'd meet at the stone lion in front of the entrance to the New York Public Library on Fifth Avenue, and from there we could walk to Central Park.

Unfortunately, I had forgotten that there were two stone lions guarding the entrance, one on the left and the other on the right of the broad stone stairway. I don't know which one of us arrived first; we might have come at the same time. I know that when I arrived, choosing the one on the right, she was not there, and I assumed that she was still on the way from Brentano's. I began pacing up and down impatiently, keeping watch on the surging homebound crowds.

It was five o'clock, the height of the rush hour for people leaving their offices. It was another warm day. A number of people were sitting on the steps that led up to the heavy revolving door of the library, mostly students taking a breather from their studies inside, some nibbling on sandwiches or sipping from containers of coffee.

Almost half an hour passed, and my impatience grew, and with it my disappointment. I had begun to think she had stood me up or had forgotten altogether about the appointment, or perhaps had never intended to keep it in the first place. My thoughts were mingled with a touch of disgust. Nevertheless, I kept on pacing in front of my lion.

She was doing the same thing in front of the lion on the far left, and thinking pretty much the same things, with the same growing disgust. It was fortunate that we both decided to give up at the same time and turned away simultaneously, as suddenly we came face-to-face. We stopped and stared at each other unbelievingly, but with unmistakable relief and delight.

"Hello," I said awkwardly.

"Hello," she said with the same awkwardness.

We shook hands, both of us very formal and not quite knowing each other fully, but as we discovered why we hadn't met on time, we broke into laughter, and all the stiffness vanished. As we walked up Fifth Avenue in the direction of the park she tucked her hand into my arm.

It was dance night that night; I held her close as we danced, and she did not seem to mind. We talked, too, and felt the same warmth that we had on our first meeting Saturday night. At one point we stopped for some refreshment, and I bought a bottle of soda for each of us. She wanted to pay for hers, but I wouldn't let her. I had come prepared this time with enough money given by my mother to pay for my subway fare and these two bottles of soda. We sat on a bench and drank. I had a raging thirst and drank mine in seconds. She had barely taken a few sips from hers and offered me her bottle, and after some hesitation I accepted, but only on condition that she share it with me.

So we spent the next few minutes passing the bottle from one to the other, until finally it was empty, and then after lifting my arm behind her to throw the empty bottle into a garbage can I let my hand drop around her and kissed her, and this time she didn't turn her head aside.

It was the start of many nights like this. The dance nights alternated with band concerts, and we went to all of them. She'd been going to night college and to modern dance classes before she met me, but she gave all that up to be with me, and there was hardly a single night that we did not meet. I had no money. I couldn't take her to a movie or a play unless I let her pay. She offered to do so a number of times, but I couldn't bring myself to let her. It really didn't matter so long as we were together, and the park with its concerts and dances was a perfect place for us.

There was boat rowing also on the lake. I loved to row, but it cost a quarter to rent a boat for an hour, and I did not have a quarter. One day, I recall, we were strolling alongside the lake and were not far from the bathhouse when Ruby cried, "Oh, look!"

She pointed downward, and there on the grass was a shiny coin. I stooped quickly and picked it up. It was a quarter, the exact amount I had been longing for to rent a boat. I was delighted, and Ruby was pleased too. We lost no time going to the boathouse and getting into one of the rowboats.

Not until many years later, long after we had been married, did I remember this incident and realize where that quarter had come from. Ruby denied it, feigning absolute innocence, but I knew the coin had come from her purse—she'd tossed it there quickly onto the grass without my seeing it. It was just another one of the lovely things about her.

As the two of us remembered these things, we saw a lot of the sadness in them, but we also laughed often over some of the things that had happened to us during this time—for instance, the time we had gone to a party at the house of some friends in downtown Manhattan. It was a small apartment and it was crowded with people and suffocatingly hot, and we were both very uncomfortable and decided to leave and go to Central Park. It had grown dark and outdoors it was a bit cooler than the apartment, and we walked, glad to be free of the noise and packed people of the apartment.

The distance to the park was considerable, but that didn't matter to us. We both loved walking, and it felt good to be able to stretch our legs. But we had gone a fair distance when Ruby slowed down and began to show signs of discomfort. I asked her what was the trouble.

"It's this damned girdle," she said.

In the fashion of the day, she wore a girdle, which also served as a garter belt to hold up silk stockings. With the heat adding to its tightness, she was having difficulty walking.

"Can't you take it off?" I asked.

She looked around. The idea appealed to her, but we were on a main street and there were cars passing and some pedestrians. "How am I going to do that?" she murmured.

I looked around too. It so happened that just ahead of us there was an old, historic church with a graveyard in which were buried soldiers from the Revolutionary War. We had been there before and had seen the stumps of gravestones that were left, on which the names were almost obliterated. I pointed it out to her and suggested she go in there, where nobody from the street could see her, and take the troublesome girdle off. I'd stand outside on the street and keep guard to make sure no one went into the graveyard.

She agreed, and we walked to the church and Ruby disappeared into the darkness of the graveyard. I waited. A few people went by, and after about ten minutes Ruby returned looking relieved.

"Oh, it's so good to be without it. Now I can really walk."

"Where's the girdle?" I asked.

She had come out with empty hands. She looked at them startled, as if just realizing it. "Oh, I forgot it," she said, and started to go back, then halted. "But what will I do with it?" she said. "My pocket-book isn't big enough to fit it in, and I can't walk through the streets and go to the dance holding a girdle in my hands."

"Will it fit in one of my pants pockets?" I asked.

She shook her head, frowning. "I don't want to lose the girdle," she said. "It happens to be the only one I have; my other is torn, and I meant to buy another one but didn't get around to it. And I'll need it for work tomorrow. Maybe I should just leave it where it is and we can pick it up on the way back."

That sounded like the best idea to me, and I asked, "Where did you put it?"

"It's hanging on a gravestone," she said.

We looked at each other for a moment, then laughed. "I don't think the old soldier will mind," I said.

"I hope not," she said. Suddenly she became serious again. "It does seem sort of sacrilegious, doesn't it?" she said.

"I wouldn't worry about it," I said, and I put my arm around her and led her on. After a few steps, still thinking about it, I said, "But if he happens to wake up it'll give him a bit of a shock."

Then we couldn't help it. We laughed hysterically almost all the way to Central Park.

We danced until midnight, when the band stopped playing and everybody left the hall. I took Ruby home on the subway, and it was just as we reached the apartment house where she lived with her mother and brother that she suddenly burst out, "Oh, my God, we forgot the girdle."

"It's safe," I said. "Nobody's going to take it, and you can pick it up on your way to work tomorrow. Only this time take a bag big enough to put it in."

"But I need it to get dressed for work tomorrow," she mourned.

There was only one thing to do. "Go upstairs and wait there. I'll go get it now and bring it back to you."

"Oh, you poor darling," she said. "I hate to make you do this."

I did it anyway. I went back to the graveyard, took the girdle off the gravestone, and rolled it up in my hands as best I could, finding it certainly did not fit into one of my pockets. Clutching it firmly, I got onto a subway to return to Brooklyn. Even at this time of night the subway was packed with people, and I was not able to get a seat. I had to stand, hanging on a strap with one hand and holding the rolled-up girdle with the other.

The train hadn't gone far when I heard a giggling sound. I looked down. Seated in front of me were two nuns. Their eyes were on the girdle in my hand, and they were trying to stifle their giggles. One of the garter straps was hanging down and almost touching the nun on my left. Other passengers seated on either side of the nuns were noticing too, and I heard some laughter.

With my cheeks blazing, I turned away from where I had been standing and stumbled out of the car altogether. I found a spot in another, half-empty car where I could be alone until I reached my station. Ruby was waiting for me inside the apartment anxiously, and she gave a sigh of relief when she opened the door and saw the girdle in my hand. She threw her arms around my neck and kissed me gratefully. She wanted me to come in and let her make some coffee, but it was late and I saw she was very tired and would have to get up early to go to work in the morning, so I begged off and hurried out, anxious to get home.

Dawn was just breaking when I arrived in the Bronx, tired out from all the subway riding I'd done but not minding it, and thinking she was the only girl I'd have done it for. I loved her very much.

There are many such sweet moments of that early period in our lives when we were just discovering each other and Central Park was our playground, virtually our second home. I have no doubt that time will dim most of them, but there is one I am sure that will linger on, perhaps forever, and that is the time, one brilliant moonlit night, when Ruby and I sat listening to a band concert in the park, and while the rest of the huge audience sat in deep silence enthralled by the music, we were restless and had to get up and slip away.

We held hands and went strolling along a dark path alongside the lake, watching the moonlight shimmering in the water, then turning our heads to see for the first time the startling beauty of our golden willow. We went up close to it, breathless, and I parted its drooping branches and we went inside. It was like walking into a cathedral, with its immense height and deep silence. In the distance, faintly, we could hear the music of the band playing, and I put my arms around Ruby and we sank down to a bed of moss and rotted leaves that gave off a rich loamy smell of earth, and we lay there for a long time in each other's arms, closer with our love than we had ever been before.

Golden willows would always bring that beautiful moment back to us, and the one we planted in our garden at the back of the house did for many years. Its loss was a tragedy to us, and while I made a mistake when I talked Ruby out of planting another one, I am glad now that I came to the realization that even if we could not see it, others could, and it would be as beautiful and as meaningful to them as it had been to us.

I go often to the little memorial park that I have created. I can make it easily with my walker, and I sit on the bench and rest and look at my trees: the big one that is for our friends, the little growing one that is for Ruby and me.

There is one more touch that I have added to make it all complete. This is a bronze plaque that I had made for the bench. It has the names of Ruby and myself inscribed on it, and underneath are the words that express my feelings about Ruby and our life together. They come from the immortal Helen Keller, who more than anyone knew the true meaning of love.

What we once enjoyed and deeply loved,
we can never lose,
for all that we love deeply becomes part of us.

Acknowledgments

I am deeply indebted to a number of people for the help they gave me in making this book possible. To my editor, Jill Schwartzman, for her valuable suggestions, and to her predecessor, Robin Rolewicz, whose enthusiasm in the initial stages of the book gave me the validation I needed. To my daughter Adraenne for her apt criticisms and especially suggesting a new and more appropriate title for the book. To my son Charles for his watchdog attitude over my welfare. To my agent Dan Lazar and to the Guggenheim Fellowship for their support, which was so greatly needed. And to the many readers of my books who have written me and have asked for this one.

ABOUT THE AUTHOR

Ninety-nine-year-old HARRY BERNSTEIN immigrated to the United States with his family after World War I. He is the author of *The Invisible Wall* and *The Dream* and has been published in "My Turn" in *Newsweek*. Bernstein lives in Brick, New Jersey, where he is working on another book.

ABOUT THE TYPE

This book was set in Minion, a 1990 Adobe Originals typeface by Robert Slimbach. Minion is inspired by classical, old-style typefaces of the late Renaissance, a period of elegant, beautiful, and highly readable type designs. Created primarily for text setting, Minion combines the aesthetic and functional qualities that make text type highly readable with the versatility of digital technology.